AMERICAN ISSUES

DEBATED

GUN CONTROL

AMERICAN ISSUES

DEBATED

GUN CONTROL

Herbert M. Levine

RSVP

RAINTREE
STECK-VAUGHN
P U B L I S H E R S
The Steck-Vaughn Company

Austin, Texas

For Bob and Roberta Dinerstein

Published by Raintree Steck-Vaughn Publishers, an imprint of Steck-Vaughn Company
Publishing Director: Walter Kossmann
Graphic Design & Project Management: Gino Coverty
Editors: Kathy DeVico, Shirley Shalit
Photo Editor: Margie Foster
Electronic Production: Gino Coverty

Library of Congress Cataloging-in-Publication Data
Levine, Herbert M.
Gun Control / Herbert M. Levine.
p. cm.—(American issues debated)
Includes bibliographical references and index.
Summary: Provides information on both sides of the gun control issue,
discussing crime, suicides, accidents, the Constitution, and government regulations.
ISBN 0-8172-4351-8
1. Gun control--United States-- Juvenile literature.
[1. Gun control.]   I. Title.   II. Series.
HV7436.L49   1998
363.3'3'0973--dc21   97-12423
                                    CIP
                                    AC

Printed and Bound in the United States
1 2 3 4 5 6 7 8 9 0 LB 01 00 99 98 97

Acknowledgments
I am grateful for the assistance of the late Jack Korsower, who provided me with information about the technical aspects of firearms. I also appreciate the expert guidance of Walter Kossmann and the careful copyediting of Shirley Shalit.—H.L.

Photograph Acknowledgments
p. 7 © Mark Newman/PhotoEdit; p. 10 © Bob Daemmrich/Sygma; p. 13 Corbis-Bettmann; p. 14 © Steve Winter/Black Star; p. 17 Courtesy Handgun Control, Inc.; p. 20 © Bob Crandall/Stock Boston; p. 23 © Steve Leonard/Black Star; p. 32 © David Young-Wolfe/PhotoEdit; p. 34 © Spencer Grant/Gamma Liaision; p. 41 © Mark Richards/PhotoEdit; p. 42 © Hemsey/Gamma-Liaison; p. 50 © Roy Morsch/The Stock Market; p. 53 © Sygma; p. 56 The Granger Collection; p. 62 Culver Pictures; p. 63 The Granger Collection; p. 69 Corbis-Bettmann; p. 71 (top right) The Granger Collection, (lower left) National Portrait Gallery, The Smithsonian Institution; p. 78 Lisa Quinones /Black Star; p. 82 © Bob Daemmrich/Sygma; p. 87 © Steve Winter/Black Star; p. 88 Courtesy Smith & Wesson; pp. 90, 96, Corbis-Bettmann; p. 103 W. B. Spunbarg/PhotoEdit; p. 108 Corbis-Bettmann; p.111 © Ernest Bazan/Gamma-Liaison; p. 113 © Gamma-Liaison; p. 115 © Terry Ashe/Gamma-Liaison.

CONTENTS

Chapter 1
INTRODUCTION: FIREARMS IN AMERICA

When young Americans go to school in many cities, often the first familiar person they meet is not their teacher, principal, or librarian, but, rather, the guard who monitors the metal detector at the entrance to the school. The guard is searching for weapons—principally guns—that students may be illegally carrying with them.

The idea of placing a metal detector at a school entrance is a strange thought for many parents to accept. They remember that when they were students, school was a safe haven for learning. But now, parents willingly welcome the metal detectors because they know that guns can turn a school into a dangerous place for children. Parental fears for the safety of children are based on the harsh cruelty of everyday life: A teenage boy shoots a classmate in a dispute about a girlfriend or because the boy wants the sports jacket that his classmate is wearing. A young drug pusher carries a gun to school for his own protection. A gang member settles a problem with a gang member of a rival group by shooting him. A boy removes a gun from his home and takes the weapon to school to impress his classmates.

The many incidents of gun use produce grim statistics for America's youth; they indicate that a child is killed by a gun every two hours in the United States. And 100,000 students carry a gun to school each day, according to a U.S. Department of Justice report.

Even private schools are not a refuge from violence. At a private, religious school in Stockton, California, on January 17, 1989, Patrick Purdy, a man with a long history of criminal activity, opened fire with an AK-47 semiautomatic weapon, killing five school-children and wounding 29 other children and one teacher before killing him-self. He fired 105 rounds, not including the single pistol bullet that he used to kill himself. Other private schools have been the scene of gun violence, too.

Although parents try to shield their children from the dangers that adults experience, some parents have not succeeded in pro-tecting their children from the gun violence that affects American society. For all Americans—regard-less of age, income, race, religion, or gender—face

Metal detectors are common in many schools in the United States.

dangers from gun violence. Even some of the most famous Americans have been victims of gun violence. Firearms were the instrument of assassination in the deaths of Presidents Abraham Lincoln, James Garfield, William McKinley, and John F. Kennedy. Presidents Andrew Jackson, Theodore Roosevelt, Franklin Roosevelt, Harry Truman, Gerald Ford, and Ronald Reagan escaped assassina-tion attempts through firearms, although both Theodore Roosevelt and Ronald Reagan were wounded in these incidents. Firearms took the lives of other prominent political leaders, such as Robert Kennedy, the brother of the slain President, and Martin Luther King, Jr., the civil rights leader. The entertainment world has not been spared either. On December 8, 1980, former Beatles star John Lennon was shot in New York, and on March 31, 1995, Selena, the popular Mexican-American singer, was killed by gunshots, too.

At times, the incidents of gun use gain public attention not because of the celebrities who are targets but rather because of the scale or unusual character of the shooting incidents. Some of the most violent cases of recent years are:

> • On October 16, 1991, George Hennard crashed his pickup truck into Luby's Cafeteria in Killeen, Texas, and opened fire. He killed 22 people instantly and wounded 20 others before killing himself.

> • On October 17, 1992, Yoshihiro Hattori, a 16-year-old Japanese exchange student in Louisiana, mistakenly entered the wrong house on his way to a Halloween party. Rodney Peairs, the homeowner, ordered him to "Freeze!" Not understanding the warning, the student continued to advance, and Peairs shot and killed him. At the trial, Peairs's attorney argued that his client reacted to a seemingly threatening attack and the death was justifiable. On May 23, 1993, Peairs was acquitted of manslaughter.

> • On December 7, 1993, Colin Ferguson opened fire on a crowded Long Island Railroad commuter train. He declared war on "whites, Asians, and 'Uncle Tom' Negroes." He killed six people and wounded 19.

Although gun violence takes a heavy toll both in the lives of its victims and in the quality of life of the victims' relatives and friends, many of the stories of the victims do not capture the headlines on page 1 of the newspapers. Each gun violence statistic is a page 1 story to the loved ones of the victims, however. Of the 24,526 homicides in the United States in 1993, an estimated 69.6 percent were committed with firearms. And thousands of other Americans are wounded from gunshots, often with long-term effects on health. To put the statistics into a context, every two years more Americans die from firearms injuries in the United States than were killed in the entire Vietnam War. And as writer Osha Gray Davidson calculates: "Since 1933, more Americans have died from gun wounds here at home than in all the wars our country has been involved in since—and including—the American Revolution."

Criminal activity, then, takes a heavy toll in human life. But guns kill and maim not only because of crime but also because of suicides and accidents. In firearm fatalities, more people die from suicides than from homicides. In 1991, for example, firearms were involved in 18,547 suicides compared to 17,763 homicides, not an unusual year as far as this kind of pattern is concerned. And firearms cause fatalities unintentionally through accidents, either by misfiring of weapons, inaccurate shooting, carelessness, or recklessness.

Although Americans use firearms in ways that are criminal or sinister, they also employ guns in ways that are often regarded as law-abiding and good. Foremost in this regard is the fact that they use firearms for self-protection. Americans can use firearms for self-protection largely because in many communities firearms are easy to get and can be bought at affordable prices. So abundant is the supply of guns in the United States that the nation has more guns in civilian hands than any other country in the world. One out of every two American households has a gun, and one out of every four households has a handgun. Americans bought almost as many handguns in 1994 (two million) as fax machines. The Bureau of Alcohol, Tobacco and Firearms (ATF), the federal bureau responsible for enforcing federal gun laws, estimates that as of 1992, approximately 212 million firearms were available for sale to or were possessed by civilians in the United States.

The approximate breakdown is as follows: 72 million handguns (mostly pistols, revolvers, derringers), 76 million rifles, and 64 million shotguns. Generally, in the United States, one to two million handguns are manufactured each year, along with one million rifles and fewer than one million shotguns. Annual imports are 200,000 to

400,000 handguns, 200,000 rifles, and 100,000 to 200,000 shotguns. The retail price of guns varies—from $50 for poor-quality guns to more than $1,500 for high-quality rifles or shotguns.

Given the size, cost, and availability of weapons, it is not surprising that criminals are more frightened of being shot by civilians than they are of being shot by the police. The availability of guns is made easy in part because of the character of the firearms distribution system. In that system, no one may legally purchase firearms from a manufacturer and distribute them into the general population without first obtaining a Type 1 Federal Firearms License (FFL), issued by the ATF of the U.S. Department of the Treasury. With an FFL, a dealer can ship and receive firearms and ammunition by common carrier (for example, a freight company) in quantity and at quantity-price discounts.

People who hold these licenses are dealers typically operating out of their homes (commonly called "kitchen-table dealers") rather than commercial enterprises operating storefront businesses (commonly

There are about 100,000 legal gun dealers in the United States.

called "stocking dealers"). Since 1994, the fees for licensed dealers are $200 for three years, and a renewal of license costs $90 for three years. (Prior to 1994, the fee for a Type 1 FFL was $30 for three years.)

The number of places to purchase firearms legally is high. According to the ATF, as of December 1996, 124,286 Americans held federal firearms licenses. Gun dealers held all but approximately 24,000 of these licenses. There has, however, been a sharp drop in the number of federal firearms licenses in recent years. In 1993, there were approximately 287,000 federal firearms licenses. The drop in licenses between 1993 and 1996 was credited to new laws, regulations, and enforcement policies adopted since 1993. The ATF expects the number of licenses to fall even further. Still, criminals who do not want to buy guns legally obtain them by stealing them or buying them "on the street."

In addition to using guns for self-protection, Americans use firearms for recreational purposes. More than 15 million Americans engage in hunting, and most of them use firearms for their sport. Many Americans use guns in sport shooting, which includes formal target shooting (such as skeet or trapshooting) and the shooting of paper targets. Sport shooting also includes informal target shooting, such as "plinking"—the shooting of tin cans and natural inanimate targets found in the woods. It has been said that firearms are the most commonly owned piece of sporting equipment in the United States with the exception of pairs of sneakers.

With a use for guns in crime, self-protection, and recreation, Americans have developed a relationship to guns unlike that of any other advanced industrial society. This relationship comes from a social and cultural tradition steeped in the use and appreciation of guns. That tradition is based on an early historical reliance on guns for hunting and on the role of guns in colonial experience, the Revolutionary War, and frontier history. It is also based on the place that guns have in American popular culture. Early settlers in the New World, as early America was called, relied on firearms to hunt animals for supplying food and for developing a rich fur industry. As the colonists moved westward, they continued to hunt. Frontier conditions were dangerous as colonists faced military threats from Native Americans and foreign nations. Because early colonial communities were relatively poor and unable to finance a professional army, the colonists had to supply their own weapons and ammunition. Moreover, the colonists themselves mobilized as a militia (armed force of citizen soldiers who may be called to service during emergencies) when the community was in danger.

The gun was important in the expansion of the new nation on the western frontier. Most of the fighting pitted the U.S. cavalry against Native Americans. But the amount of gunfighting that many Americans associate with the West—most notably shootouts and gunfights—was limited. As historian Richard Shenkman notes: "The truth is many more people have died in Hollywood westerns than ever died on the real frontier (Indian wars considered apart)." Popular culture in America reflects a concern, sometimes even a love, for guns. For generations, novels and movies depicted gunfighting in the Old West as common and heroic.

One of the most popular movie series of recent years was the Clint Eastwood films featuring Detective Harry Callahan, or "Dirty Harry" as he was called, relying on his .44 Magnum to fight criminals. Other movie series, such as *Rambo*, *Lethal Weapon*, and *Die Hard*, have popularized assault weapons. And television has featured assault weapons in series like "Miami Vice." Even President Bill Clinton, an advocate of gun control, reflected the sentiment of the gun culture when he said: "I can still remember the first day when I was a little boy out in the country, putting the can on top of a fence post and shooting a .22 at it. I can well remember the first time I pulled a trigger on a .410 shotgun, because I was too little to hold a .2-gauge. This is part of the culture of a big part of America."

While the gun culture shows that Americans are fascinated with guns, they are sharply divided about whether government should set strict regulations over the sale, possession, and use of guns. Although Americans debated gun control as early as the 19th century, the

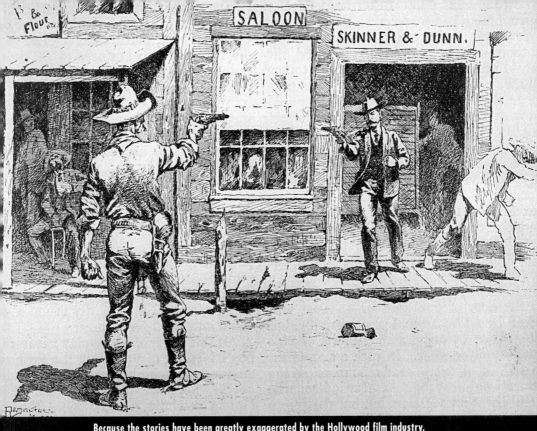

Because the stories have been greatly exaggerated by the Hollywood film industry, many Americans associate gunfights with the West.

issues have been more sharply drawn since the 1960s mostly as a result of the assassinations of public figures, an increase in the number of weapons that are owned by Americans, horrifying incidents of mass gun violence that have captured national attention, a high toll of lives lost because of gunfire particularly in inner cities, and the increased firepower of modern weapons.

Advocates of gun control call for greater regulation of guns in American life. They argue that guns are more dangerous than other products in causing death and injury in crimes, suicides, and accidents. They say that alternatives to gun possession, such as reliance on police and effective security systems, would provide the same or even better safety than guns offer. They see guns as posing a national health problem that needs to be resolved.

Although agreeing that the ownership and use of firearms need to be regulated, gun control advocates differ among themselves about how they should be regulated. Some call for banning possession of all handguns. Others support less strict measures, such as mandatory waiting periods to purchase guns, restrictions on the type of weapons that a person can purchase, and limitations on the number of gun dealers.

Opponents of gun control call for no—or limited—regulation of guns in American life. They argue that guns are not the problem. They say: "Guns don't kill; people kill." Imposing bans or regulations

Members of the NRA argue that the Second Amendment assures every individual a right to possess arms.

on the possession of guns, they contend, will only harm law-abiding citizens because criminals are not bound by laws anyway. Gun regulation in this way of thinking will increase crime because criminals will feel free to act without fear of challenge by their victims. Critics of gun control say that in the absence of guns, people who want to commit suicide will find another way to take their own lives. Moreover, they contend that the number of people who are victims of gun accidents is small and can be reduced even further with more training and education about the safe handling of weapons.

In general, opponents of gun control favor repealing many of the existing gun control laws. They oppose most attempts to restrict the citizens' right to buy and own weapons of their choice. They have been particularly critical of the ATF as a result of the agency's efforts to enforce federal gun laws. A fund-raising letter of the National Rifle Association (NRA), a pro-gun organization, referred to the ATF as "jackbooted government thugs," a reference suggesting a cruel police force of a dictatorship. The letter produced so much controversy that the executive vice president of the NRA spoke against it.

Although the debate over guns is often argued on the basis of support or opposition to gun control, the term gun control is an inaccurate wording to describe the controversy. In this regard, even most opponents of "gun control" favor laws that prevent felons—people convicted of serious crimes—from possessing guns. However, the term gun control is used in this book in its more popular meaning to signify support for government restrictions on gun sales, ownership, and use.

The debate over guns is expressed most prominently by representatives of private organizations and their supporters in and out of government. Supporters of limited government involvement in gun matters make up what is called the "gun lobby." A lobby is a group that attempts to influence the content of government laws and the policies of government agencies. The NRA is the principal representative of the gun lobby. Among other organizations that are supportive of many of the views of the NRA are Citizens Committee for the Right to Keep and Bear Arms, Gun Owners Incorporated (formerly Gun Owners of America), and the Second Amendment Foundation. Other major supporters of many of the views of the gun lobby are gun manufacturers and gun dealers.

The leading supporter of gun control is Handgun Control, Inc. (HCI). Among other organizations that favor gun control are the Center to Prevent Handgun Violence, Coalition to Stop Gun Violence (formerly the National Coalition to Ban Handguns), Educational Fund to Ban Handgun Violence, and Violence Policy Center. Although sharing a commitment for gun control, these organizations have differences over specific policies. For example, the Coalition to Stop Gun Violence favors a ban on the private possession of handguns but HCI does not. Some police organizations have been particularly concerned with issues involving assault weapons and ammunition that can pierce bulletproof vests.

The gun lobby and its opponents attempt to influence law and public policy at the national, state, and local level. Often, the debate over gun control deals with the meaning of the Second Amendment to the Constitution, which states: "A well regulated Militia, being necessary to the security of a free State, the right of the people to keep and bear Arms shall not be infringed [violated]." Supporters of gun control argue that the Second Amendment assures the individual states of the United States the right to form militias. Opponents of gun control argue that the Second Amendment, as part of the Bill of Rights, assures every individual a right to possess arms. The debate over the meaning of the Second Amendment is a continuing one.

The major public policy battles are fought over federal, state, and local laws dealing with gun control. Federal gun control laws are few in number and were not enacted until the 20th century. The federal laws cover many subjects, including banning the sale of certain kinds of guns (such as machine guns, some assault weapons, and firearms that cannot be detected by security devices), regulating the sale of guns and licensing of dealers, and imposing a five-day waiting period for citizens to purchase a handgun.

IN 1992, HANDGUNS KILLED
33 PEOPLE IN GREAT BRITAIN
36 IN SWEDEN
97 IN SWITZERLAND
60 IN JAPAN
13 IN AUSTRALIA
128 IN CANADA
AND 13,220 IN THE UNITED STATES.

GOD BLESS AMERICA.

Help stop handgun violence.
Call 1-900-860-8787.
A letter will be sent to Congress in your name,
urging support of stronger federal handgun laws.
(The $3.75 cost of the call will appear on your phone bill.)

Handgun Control, Inc., 1225 Eye Street, N.W.
Washington, D.C. 20005

STOP HANDGUNS BEFORE THEY STOP YOU.

in public

However, state and local governments have passed more than 20,000 laws regulating guns. These laws include regulating the place and manner for people to sell, buy, or carry firearms, imposing strong penalties for crimes committed with a firearm, forbidding some kinds of individuals (for example, criminals convicted of serious crimes) from owning guns, granting licenses to own guns, registering guns, and banning guns.

The debate over gun control is often made in emotional terms. Both sides identify their opponents as "outside the mainstream." Some gun control advocates portray opponents as psychopaths (that is, people with personality disorders), or "gun nuts," who are insensitive to the dangers that guns pose to men, women, and children. Opponents of gun control often view their critics as liberals who are insensitive to the needs of ordinary people and who want to make citizens defenseless against criminals.

Efforts at reaching an intelligent opinion on the subject of gun control face many problems, most notably problems that include agreeing on definitions of key terms of discussion, accepting the facts about the reasons for crime and suicides, evaluating the statistics about gun use, and analyzing the constitutional meaning of the Second Amendment. This book offers readers an opportunity to consider which side makes the better case on gun control.

Chapter 2
GUNS AND AMMUNITION

Guns have been a feature of peoples and cultures for hundreds of years. Over the centuries, changes in the technology of guns have improved their firepower, accuracy, range, and effectiveness. Technological change has also advanced the construction of bullets in a manner that affects the damage that ammunition can cause to a shooter's target. Because a study of gun control requires an understanding of guns and ammunition, this chapter provides some essential facts on this subject.

A dictionary might define a gun as a mechanical device that throws one or more objects outward, usually through a tube or barrel. Most guns use a gunpowder charge or some other substance capable of igniting or burning to power the bullet, and these weapons are known as firearms. Some weapons are powered not by gunpowder but rather by such elements as steam, compressed air, carbon dioxide, or spring pressure.

Most guns shoot bullets, which are soft lead pellets. But some guns shoot objects other than bullets, for example, darts. And shotguns, which are described on page 20, shoot hundreds of pellets contained in a shell with each firing of the weapon. Shotgun ammunition is called "shot."

One way to distinguish guns is to classify them into long guns and handguns. A long gun is any firearm meant to be fired from the shoulder. There are two kinds of long guns: shotguns and rifles.

A shotgun is often described in terms of "gauge" (or "bore" in Great Britain). Gauge is the diameter of a shotgun barrel as measured in the number of lead balls of a size fitting the barrel that can be made from a pound of lead. Shotgun barrels are usually smooth inside. Shotguns are usually fired at a moving target (or targets). Because they release many pellets with each firing, shotguns are pointed rather than precisely aimed at their target. Shotgun ammunition does not have the capability of traveling long distances. In general, shotguns are effective only over a distance of 40 yards with a maximum effective distance of about 100 yards under certain conditions. Because they are long guns, shotguns are not easily concealed. However, it is possible to saw off the barrel of a shotgun to produce a gun that can easily be carried in a concealed manner. It is illegal in the United States to manufacture or own sawed-off shotguns.

Because of their length, shotguns and rifles are not easily concealed.

A rifle is a firearm with a rifled barrel fitted with a stock intended to be held against the shoulder. A rifled barrel means that the barrel contains spiral grooves. As a bullet goes through the barrel of a gun, these grooved spirals cause the bullet to spin. The longer the barrel and the tighter the spiral, the faster the spin of the bullet. A bullet fired from a rifle moves more rapidly than a bullet fired from a handgun. Rifles are usually more accurate than handguns. Rifles are designed for precision shooting. They are capable of hitting targets at longer ranges than shotguns and handguns. Rifles can hit targets hundreds of yards away, but most uses of rifles in hunting and military combat occur in a range from 150 to 300 yards. Unlike shotguns, rifles are usually fired from a stationary rather than a moving position.

Handguns are small firearms, with barrels usually varying in length between two and eight inches. They are sometimes called pistols. They are designed to be fired with one or both hands. Handguns are often easily concealed because they are small. Also complicating the ability to detect handguns is the fact that some handguns have plastic components. Some observers say that guards monitoring metal-detector devices sometimes have difficulty in detecting guns with plastic parts, but this view is strongly challenged by opponents of gun control.

Revolvers are the simplest kind of handguns. (Some writers do not identify revolvers as pistols.) Depending upon the kind of revolver, a cylinder (revolving chamber) holds five or six cartridges (the cases that hold the charge for a gun), which may be fired in succession. When the gun is fired, the revolving chamber moves and a new cartridge is put in place to be shot. After the five or six cartridges have been fired, new cartridges must be installed before a person can begin to shoot again. Single-action revolvers are guns in which one shot is loaded manually (by hand) at a time. Double-action revolvers can be fired by merely pulling the trigger.

One kind of handgun that has received attention is the so-called "Saturday night special." This weapon is generally an inexpensive and poorly made handgun that is easily concealed. Another notable handgun is the .44 Magnum revolver. (See Chapter 1.) It is a high-powered firearm that is capable of firing a bullet that travels at a speed nearly twice as fast as the average revolver bullet. Its cylinder holds six cartridges. The impact of its bullet can be so severe that the bullet usually passes directly through a target and hits whatever is behind it.

Firearms can be classified as single-shot, manual repeaters, semiautomatics, or automatics. A single-shot is a gun in which one shot is loaded by hand at one time for each firing (see page 21). A repeater is a gun capable of being fired several times without reloading. The person who fires a manual repeater, however, must do everything by hand (move the lever, bolt, or pump) to throw out the spent (used) cartridge and bring a new cartridge from the compartment in which cartridges are held to the firing chamber. A semiautomatic firearm requires the shooter to pull the trigger for each shot that is fired. An automatic firearm fires continuously with the pressing of the trigger.

The semiautomatic and automatic throw out the spent cartridge case and, without any manual intervention, place a new cartridge into the chamber. Unlike the revolver, the semiautomatic and automatic firearm cartridges are stacked in a container, called a magazine or a clip, which is usually located within the gun's handle or grip. Semiautomatic handguns are sometimes called "self-loaders," "automatics," or "auto pistols."

Other terms needing definitions in any consideration of issues of gun control are machine guns, submachine guns, and assault weapons. A machine gun is an automatic weapon that fires rifle ammunition. Ammunition for machine guns is fed by either belts or clips. A submachine gun is a fully automatic weapon that fires pistol ammunition. The tommy gun is a submachine gun made famous in the gangland crimes of the 1930s. It is named for its inventor, John T. Thompson.

The term assault weapons is used to describe military-style or police-style weapons. Some writers describe assault weapons only as

A wide variety of automatic and semiautomatic firearms are available for sale today.

automatic firearms and exclude semiautomatics, but others define the term to be more inclusive of different kinds of firearms. Writer Michael Newton notes: "Despite recent misuse of the term in media reports, semiautomatic arms are not 'assault' weapons." But political scientist Robert J. Spitzer writes: "Assault-style semiautomatic weapons are distinguished from others in that they have large clips holding 20-30 bullets, are more compact in design, have barrels under 20 inches in length, take intermediate-sized cartridges, include extensive use of stampings and plastics, weigh 6-10 pounds, and are designed for military use. In addition, they have pistol grips, grenade launchers, and bayonet fittings."

Even the term military requires careful attention when applied to firearms. Military firearms are not necessarily more damage-producing than civilian weapons. In this regard, many military rifles are designed to wound rather than kill, because a wounded soldier requires medical attention and the use of an enemy's resources for medical care.

As writer David B. Kopel notes, the AR-15 Sporter and the semiautomatic Kalashnikov rifle look horrible, but they are far less lethal (capable of causing death) than a standard hunting rifle such as the Springfield bolt action .30-'06. And military bullets are more likely to pass through a body, whereas hunting bullets are designed to deform within the body, to not exit, and to transfer all their kinetic energy (energy associated with motion) to the target. Bullet wounds from hunting rifles are, then, more severe than bullet wounds from military rifles.

An understanding of firearms requires an awareness of how complicated it may be to identify certain kinds of guns. In this regard, manufacturers of firearms have been resourceful in producing spare parts that can change the character of weapons. A manufacturer may comply with the law in producing a firearm that is not an automatic weapon. But the same manufacturer (or some other manufacturer) may produce a spare part, which with some minor adjustment can be added to an existing semiautomatic to convert it to an automatic weapon. In fact, most semiautomatic guns can be modified in this manner. In one case, gun owners required only a paper clip to convert a semiautomatic gun into an automatic gun.

With proper care, a firearm can last for many years. When Squeaky Fromm attempted to assassinate President Gerald Ford in 1975, she used a handgun manufactured in 1911. Vincent Foster, President Clinton's deputy White House counsel, committed suicide in 1993 with a .38-caliber Army Colt revolver manufactured in 1913. And dealers keep guns in serviceable use that were manufactured centuries ago. By all accounts, many guns manufactured in the early 20th century are in use today.

A few words about ammunition are necessary when discussing firearms. A bullet is the tip of a cartridge that is loaded into a gun. The cartridge contains gunpowder at the rear of the bullet and a primer (a sparking device). When a firing pin in a gun strikes the primer, then the primer ignites the gunpowder. Unlike gasoline when ignited, the gunpowder burns slowly, causing gas to build up. The gunpowder does not explode. The gas pressure then propels the bullet on its course. The damage caused by a bullet depends on the location in the body where the bullet hits, the size and speed of the bullet, and the injury to the core of tissue surrounding the bullet track.

Caliber refers to the diameter of a bullet measured in decimals of an inch. The weapon is described in terms of the caliber. A .22 caliber weapon is a firearm that uses bullets that are .22 inches in diameter. (In some firearms, however, measurement is made according to the metric system. The 6 mm [millimeter] Remington and 7 mm Mauser are two examples.)

While a .22 caliber gun is smaller than a .45 caliber gun, it can be just as lethal. Sirhan Sirhan used a .22 caliber bullet to assassinate Robert Kennedy. And John Hinckley used the same kind of bullet in his attempted assassination of Ronald Reagan.

Although half of American households have guns, most of these have long guns, not handguns. According to one report, only one-seventh of households with guns have only handguns. But handguns are the firearms that are most commonly used in crimes committed with firearms.

Chapter 3
GUNS AND CRIME

Debate: Will Gun Control Reduce Crime?

Violent crime is a real fear of every American, no matter how rich or poor. Because guns play such a major role in violent crime, a number of government officials and private citizens call for gun control as a remedy for the violence. For its part, the gun lobby argues that the problem of violent crime needs to be addressed in ways other than by gun control.

However much contending groups differ about the effectiveness of gun control as a solution to crime, they are in general agreement about the facts of violent crime. In this regard, the U.S. Department of Justice reports in its *National Crime Victimization Survey* that 43.6 million criminal victimizations occurred in the United States in 1993. (The survey defines victimization as a crime affecting one individual person or household.) Of the 4.4 million victims of rape and sexual assault, robbery, and aggravated assault (assault with the use of weapons or threat of use of weapons with the intention of inflicting injury), 1.3 million stated that they faced an offender with a firearm. And 86 percent, or 1.1 million, of these victims said that the weapon was a handgun. In 1992, about a third of all murders, robberies, and aggravated assaults reported to law-enforcement agencies were committed with firearms. These included more than 16,000 murders, 271,000 robberies, and 278,000 aggravated assaults.

Every year the *Uniform Crime Reports,* a collection of crime facts in the United States, provides the statistics about crime. The violent crime facts for 1994 show:

- 1 violent crime every 17 seconds.

- 1 murder every 23 minutes.

- 1 forcible rape every 5 minutes.

- 1 robbery every 51 seconds.

- 1 aggravated assault every 28 seconds.

Each year between 1987 and 1992 in the United States, an average of 161,000 violent crimes with a firearm resulted in injury or death. So deadly is the violence that homicide is the tenth leading cause of death in the United States. Moreover, the United States has the highest homicide rate of any Western industrialized country. In the United States, a person is shot every two minutes; and a person dies from a gunshot wound every 14 minutes.

The source of the violence tells much about American society. Most violence occurs from arguments among people who know each other and not from criminal activities, such as robbery. Violence between family members and acquaintances accounts for more than half of all homicides. The toll of violent activity is particularly high for young people. The leading cause of death for both black and white young males in America is gunshot wounds. Women are also victims. According to writer Paxton Quigley: "If you are over the age of twelve and female, be prepared to be criminally assaulted some time in your life. If you are about thirty years old now, there's a fifty-fifty chance of your being raped, robbed, or attacked."

According to the *National Crime Survey,* a source of national crime statistics prepared by the Bureau of the Census, from 1979 to

1987, surveyed victims reported that handguns were the most frequently used weapons in violent crimes of aggravated assault, robbery, and rape although handguns make up about one-fourth of the firearms in the United States. It is not surprising that the debate on gun control centers mostly on handguns.

Because firearms—particularly handguns—play such an important role in crime, gun control advocates say that a way to reduce violent crime is to restrict or regulate their sale and possession. Opponents of gun control argue that the focus on restricting or regulating guns is wrong and may in fact lead to more crime.

Number of Violent Firearm Crimes in the United States Reported to the Police per 100,000 Population

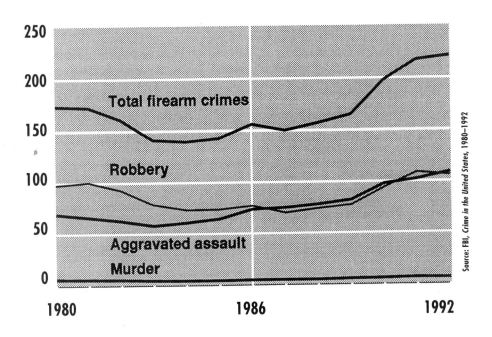

Source: FBI, Crime in the United States, 1980–1992

DEBATED:

WILL GUN CONTROL
REDUCE CRIME?

Yes. The more than 200 million guns in America have turned the entire nation into a war zone in which nobody is safe. Thousands of people who own guns use them in crime. Guns—particularly handguns—are the principal weapon used for criminal purposes. A way to reduce the level of crime is to place regulations on the sale and ownership of guns to keep them out of the hands of criminals.

Guns kill. Handguns are so hazardous that it is shocking that our consumer laws do not offer protection to our citizens. We regulate automobiles and building construction because without such rules, the public would experience great danger (such as more automobile crashes and more cave-ins of buildings). Firearms and ammunition, however, need not be regulated by the Consumer Product Safety Commission (CPSC), the federal agency that seeks to protect the public from unreasonable risk of injury associated with consumer products. The CPSC evaluates the safety of less dangerous products but lacks the legal authority to regulate dangerous firearms.

The lack of effective safety laws for guns and ammunition in the United States is a reflection of an attitude that gives special treatment to firearms. That attitude is based in part on the view that guns themselves are not dangerous. As the pro-gun advocates say: "Guns don't kill; people do." In this regard, opponents of gun control argue that anyone who blames a weapon for a crime should be blaming the criminal, instead. But as Pete Shields, a former chairman of HCI, explains in the title of his book about guns: "Guns don't die—people do."

It is true that guns don't kill, people do. But people use handguns to kill. This should come as no surprise to anyone who understands firearms because the handgun is designed for no purpose other than to kill humans.

The United States is the only democracy that does not have strict gun control laws, and the consequences of this situation show up in the form of criminal behavior. Countries with strict gun controls have less crime than the United States. Homicides are a case in point. As HCI reports, in 1992, handguns killed 33 people in Great Britain, 36 people in Sweden, 97 in Switzerland, 60 in Japan, 13 in Australia, 128 in Canada, and 13,320 in the United States.

A key study of two neighboring cities illustrates how gun control laws have a real impact on crime. Researchers conducted a study of firearm-related homicides and suicides in Seattle, Washington (in the northwestern United States), and Vancouver, British Columbia (in western Canada), which are nearby metropolitan areas. Although the cities are similar in population features and in crime, they differed in the number of guns per person and the laws that governed the possession of firearms. Vancouver had a lower handgun-related homicide rate than Seattle.

The Seattle-Vancouver study shows that gun control works. If we can find a way to sharply reduce the number of handguns in America, then we will see a reduction in violent crime. This is not to say that criminals will stop engaging in crime if handguns are unavailable to them. Hardened criminals who are determined to commit crimes will continue to do so no matter what the laws say. It would be foolish to believe otherwise.

But not all criminals are "hardened," and not all crimes are carefully planned. Some people are tempted by crime and will take advantage of an opportunity to engage in crime if an opportunity arises. Some criminologists (students of crime and criminal behavior) think that most criminals fall into this group. For those people who can be tempted in this manner, guns offer an opportunity not equaled by most other weapons to engage in violent crimes. Banning or restricting guns will prevent many people in this group of criminals from surrendering to temptation.

With gun control, people who want to engage in criminal activity would have to find some weapons other than handguns to use in committing crimes. It would be unlikely that they would choose long guns since these weapons do not contain a key feature of handguns: namely, concealability—an ability to be hidden. Criminals would turn to other small weapons, most notably knives, which are far less lethal than handguns.

Substituting knives for guns will have an impact on crime not only by strangers but also by people who know each other. Although much news media attention is given to crime among strangers, most of the firearm homicides in the United States occur among people who know each other. Often, these crimes involve members of a family who are enraged about a family matter, or unmarried people in a troubled romantic relationship. Sometimes, the anger is heightened when the parties have consumed large amounts of alcohol or drugs. In a moment of rage, a person takes a gun and kills someone with whom he or she has been arguing. If that person did not have a gun on hand, then he or she would not have killed anyone. But a gun is so deadly that homicide is a likely outcome in that situation.

If gun control laws were tough and prevented a gun from even being available at the time of such an argument, the homicide would not have occurred in many cases. Moreover, if a weapon other than a gun were used, the results would likely be less lethal.

Security. Many people keep guns in their homes because these weapons give their owners a psychological feeling of security. If something happens, such as a criminal breaking into their home, they will have a way to defend themselves and their property, they believe. Such a "feel-good" sentiment is based on illusion rather than reality, however, because the possession of a gun in the home is more dangerous to the gun owner and his or her family than it is to a criminal.

The facts of self-defense deny the illusion of self-defense. Opponents of gun control give highly doubtful figures of up to one million for the number of times an individual pulls a gun in self-defense. The objective evidence is that the number is much smaller. According to the *National Crime Survey*, about 50,000 defensive gun uses in violent crimes were reported annually between 1979 and 1985. And Philip J. Cook, a scholar who has researched the subject, estimated the annual figure at 80,000. The likelihood of using a gun in self-defense is quite small.

Having a gun in the home, then, is not much of a danger to an intruder. But it is a danger to the innocent gun owner. In an article in the *New England Journal of Medicine*, Arthur Kellerman, an emergency room physician, and his associates evaluated the impact that possession of a gun in the home has on personal security. The researchers tried to determine whether keeping a firearm in the home provides protection against crime or, instead, increases the risk of violent crime in the home. They studied homicides occurring in the homes of victims in three metropolitan areas. They also studied a group consisting of subjects matched to the victims according to neighborhood, sex, race, and age range.

They found that keeping a gun in the home was strongly and independently associated with an increased risk of homicide. Having a gun in a person's home nearly triples the likelihood of someone being killed there. "Efforts to increase home security have largely focused on preventing unwanted entry, but the greatest threat to the lives of household members appears to come from within," they write. The researchers note that the use of illicit drugs and a history of physical fights in the home are also important risk factors in domestic homicides.

The danger of firearms to their owners is also borne out by other researchers. Josh Sugarmann, executive director of the Violence Policy Center, observes: "According to federal statistics, for every time a citizen uses a handgun to kill a criminal, 118 innocent lives are ended in handgun murders, suicides, and accidents. In other words, whenever handguns are around, the 'right hands' have a tendency to turn into the 'wrong hands.'"

When a gun is kept in a home, there is always the danger of it falling into the wrong hands.

Accidents from guns present another danger to the owners of guns. (See Chapter 4.) Often, carelessness results in tragedy. In a study appearing in the *Journal of the American Medical Association* in June 1992, Douglas S. Weil and David Hemenway of the Department of Health Policy and Management at the Harvard School of Public Health show that a significant number of gun owners disregard basic safety procedures. A major safety problem, they note, is that many gun owners keep their weapons loaded. The Weil/Hemenway survey of 605 individuals determined: "More than one third of the gun owners kept their gun(s) loaded either all the time (25%) or some of the time (12%). Furthermore, 53% of the people surveyed did not keep their firearms locked up." The researchers noted that handgun owners were more than twice as likely as other people who owned firearms to keep their guns loaded at least some of the time.

A study by the General Accounting Office (GAO), the investigative arm of Congress, indicates that two devices, a childproof safety mechanism and a mechanism that shows whether a gun is loaded, could reduce accidental fatalities by about 31 percent. But many opponents of gun control oppose laws that would require the installation of these devices.

Accidents aside, it is a mistake to believe that having a firearm in one's home discourages burglary. Having a gun to prevent burglaries is generally unnecessary. Most burglars in the United States enter a home when they believe no one is there. It would be foolish of the burglars to look for trouble, since the danger of being seen and caught is already present. Having a gun in the home to stop a burglar is rarely of benefit to the person or persons living in the home.

Finally, from a security point of view, the possession of firearms in an innocent person's home can unintentionally lead to arming the very people whom the innocent person fears. A criminal rarely goes to a store to buy a gun for fear that the application for a gun purchase will only alert the police to the criminal's illegal activities. Many criminals seek other means to obtain their weapons. One of the means is to steal a gun from a home when the owner is away. That gun will then be used in committing crimes that may result in the death or injury of innocent people who are unknown to the legitimate owner of the gun.

Substitute weapons. An effective gun control policy would lead to a reduction in the number of deaths caused by criminal violence because guns are more dangerous than any other weapon used in crime. No doubt, criminals would look for weapons other than guns to carry out their illegal activities. The most likely substitute for guns would be knives, which are the second most dangerous weapon used in homicide. But knives are five times less likely to kill than guns.

Criminals could not effectively turn to rifles and shotguns because these firearms do not have the qualities that handguns do. Not only are handguns easily concealed, but they can attack their targets at great distances, and can be used by physically weak individuals against stronger individuals.

Alternatives. If a person is threatened by someone with a pointed gun, the best chance of survival is not to go after the person holding the weapon. In this regard, Pete Shields writes: "As police officers have said for years, the best defense against injury is to put up no defense—give them what they want, or run. This may not be like 'macho,' but it can keep you alive."

The facts show that a potential victim has a greater likelihood to survive if he or she does not resist a robbery with a lethal weapon. A person who resists a criminal is eight times more likely to be killed than one who does not.

Less dangerous alternatives to guns provide a community with greater protection than massive possession of guns. Legally permitted sanctioned street patrols are one example. Such patrols involving community members can spot suspicious criminal activities and alert police even before a crime is committed. And households can also be protected with secure locks and effective alarm systems.

One alternative to carrying a gun is learning self-defense techniques.

Women can carry nonlethal weapons, such as a chemical or pepper spray. Mace, a liquid that a person can squirt into the eyes of a would-be assailant, can be effective. Other defensive chemical and pepper sprays are also available and can furnish security. Mace will temporarily blind a person whose eyes are sprayed, thus allowing a possible victim time to get away from an assailant. Such sprays are easily available today in such places as hardware stores, shopping malls, and mail-order houses. Industry representatives say that ten million canisters (containers) of defensive chemical spray are in the hands of the police and the public. Sprays are inexpensive, too.

Women would also find an understanding of karate or other self-defense techniques to be useful against assaults. They can purchase personal alarms, which when made active, can make a loud noise that will attract attention and scare off assailants.

Practical policy. Most Americans recognize that government regulation is necessary for certain purposes. One of those purposes is public safety. Government establishes licensing requirements to drive automobiles because reckless drivers can and do cause deaths and injuries. Similarly, government regulates the sale of alcohol because of the dangers that people who consume alcoholic beverages can cause not only to themselves but to others, as well.

To be sure, laws about automobile driving and liquor sales are often ignored, but that is not an argument against the laws. More people are alive because of the laws against driving while intoxicated. Similarly, the high toll of life and limb claimed by guns each year would be lowered if strict gun control laws are enacted.

Much is made of new police tactics that allow the police to search people who are committing minor offenses. Although such tactics are resulting in a lowering of violent crime, the consequences of such action to our civil liberties are frightening when the police violate rights of privacy. Complaints to the Civilian Complaint Review Board about police harassment increased considerably as a result of the policy. Advocates of civil liberties justly complain that the police frisking operations target minorities in poor neighborhoods and in public housing projects. But the police can be held to account by protecting people from gun violence and by respecting the civil liberties of every person.

The lives and safety of Americans are endangered not only by guns but by the illusions that innocent people have about guns. Guns kill and are more dangerous to innocent people who keep them for protection than they are to criminals. With gun control, weapons that can be substituted for guns will be far less deadly than guns. People who feel threatened can rely on means other than guns, such as the police and neighborhood patrols, to assure security for themselves and their property. Gun control is a practical policy to adopt in the United States provided that the American people have the will to pass the laws necessary to end the bloodbath that the nation experiences every year.

No. Before the invention of guns, people were killing each other. Poisons, arrows, swords, rocks, and slingshots killed and maimed in ancient times, just as guns do today. If ancient people rejected those weapons, they would surely have found other ways to kill and plunder. Similarly today, even if guns did not exist, criminals would find weapons other than guns to commit their crimes.

In March 1995, for example, a radical group in Japan used poison gas in an attack on the Tokyo subway system, killing 12 people and injuring more than 5,500. The same year, an explosion rocked the Alfred P. Murrah Federal Building in Oklahoma City, leaving 168 people dead including 19 children, and more than 500 others injured. The evidence is clear that the cause of crime is far more complex than can be explained by the weapons that criminals use to achieve their unjust goals.

People kill. The fact that the United States has a higher gun ownership rate and experiences more gun crimes than other countries does not mean that guns cause crime and that banning guns will reduce crime. The United States has high gun ownership for many reasons, most of which have nothing to do with the committing of crimes. And the existence of crime in America has less to do with the presence of firearms than with other factors.

Although some guns are used in crimes, most guns are not. According to Gary Kleck, a leading scholar on firearm use, only one percent of the 60 million handguns in circulation in the United States involves the criminal use of guns. Most Americans possess guns that are used for legitimate purposes. Even if one accepts the figure of ten percent of guns used for crime that is claimed by some researchers, it is clear that most Americans possess guns that are used for legitimate purposes.

If it is true that the more guns in circulation, the more criminal incidents will occur, we would expect that an increase in the number of guns would lead to an increase in the amount of violent crime. The historical pattern of gun ownership in the United States, however, shows no predictable relationship between the level of gun ownership and the amount of violence against people. The United States experienced a decline in crime and homicide rates in the 1940s, 1950s, and early 1980s at the same time that gun possession in those periods increased. Between 1937 and 1963, handgun ownership rose by about 250 percent but homicide rates fell by 35.7 percent.

Regional statistics about gun possession furnish other evidence that there is no direct relationship between the numbers of firearms and the amount of criminal violence. In the United States, firearm possession has a higher concentration in rural areas and small towns than in big cities. And yet, violent crime is a problem of big cities rather than rural areas and small towns.

We could reasonably make a case that more violence leads to more guns, rather than the other way around. For example, in the month after the Los Angeles riots of 1992, in which the police withdrew from protecting people in the face of rioting mobs, gun sales jumped 45 percent over the previous year because citizens rushed to have weapons to defend themselves in the event of future riots.

The problem of violence in the United States is not that Americans have guns but rather, that Americans are a violent people. Although it is true that Americans use guns in violence, they commit violent acts without guns, too. In fact, the rate of non-gun violent acts is also higher than the comparable rate in other democracies. Great Britain has a low homicide rate but not because of gun control laws. The murder rate in the United States was higher than the murder rate in Great Britain even before gun control laws were adopted in Great Britain. British rates of low gun crime existed when gun controls did not even exist in that country. Today, Great Britain even has a lower rate of knife homicide and killings with hands or feet than does the United States. The pattern of violent crime is similar in countries other than Great Britain, as well. America has a higher gun violence rate than Western Europe, but it has a higher violence rate of all kinds than Western Europe. Japan has a low murder rate at the same time that few people own guns in Japan. But Switzerland has a similar low murder rate although gun ownership is widespread in that European country.

A likely explanation for the differences in the rate of violence of countries owes more to the culture of a society than it does to its gun control laws. Culture may be defined as the core of traditional ideas, practices, and technology shared by a people. Japan has a low rate of violence because of Japanese culture. That is to say that Japanese people throughout the world have a low rate of violence. According to policy analyst B. Bruce-Briggs, Japanese Americans have a lower violent crime rate than do Japanese in Japan, although Japanese Americans live in a country with easy access to guns. Canada has strict gun laws and a lower firearms homicide rate than the United States. But Canada has one of the highest rates of gun ownership in the world—almost as high a rate as exists in the United States. Canada has about the same rate of long gun ownership as the United States, but the United States has more legal handguns than Canada. Canadian culture shows a respect for authority and a rejection of violence.

"My state has probably one of the highest gun ownership rates in the country," says Patrick Leahy, a Democratic senator from Vermont. "We have virtually no gun control law, and we have the second-lowest crime rate in the country."

The attempt by gun control advocates to ridicule the idea that "Guns don't kill; people do," ignores the reason that many people kill. Although most homicides are not planned, one cannot know for sure how intense the feeling of the killer is at the time of attack. If a person is intent on killing another, he or she would be likely to use a weapon until the deed was done—no matter what weapon was available.

Advocates of gun control say that many fatalities would be avoided with gun control because so many gun incidents occur as crimes of passion. The idea that people go crazy and start shooting a spouse or a child in an unusual outburst ignores the fact that most cases of family violence are not unique events. That is to say that most cases of domestic homicide are preceded by incidents of domestic violence. Prior violence is a predictor of domestic homicide. A study in Kansas City examined every domestic homicide that occurred in a single year. The police had been called to a family residence within the previous five years to break up a domestic quarrel in 85 percent of the cases. In half of the cases, the police had been there five or more times. These are not isolated events limited to Kansas City but in varying numbers affect other American cities.

A gun incident in a case of domestic violence could often be avoided if an effective criminal justice system could intervene in a violent family dispute. Unfortunately, many communities do not treat domestic abuse incidents as seriously as they should. The solution for some domestic crime, then, is to enforce domestic abuse laws, not ban guns.

Security. People often possess guns because of legitimate security fears. A *U.S. News & World Report* poll in 1994 revealed that 45 percent of gun owners, asked why they have guns, cited self-protection as one of the main reasons. The possession of guns gives these people a feeling of security. Owning a gun is a risky business, to be sure. The gun may be stolen. It may be removed by a young person and may be used to kill or injure someone accidentally. Maybe the owner or a spouse may use the gun against the other in the heat of an argument. But not having a gun is a risky business, too, particularly when one has loved ones to protect and property to defend. Individuals must have the freedom to decide for themselves whether possessing a gun is more risky than not possessing a gun.

In addition to having guns for self-protection, the possession of guns by noncriminals deters (that is, prevents or discourages) crime rather than makes it easier to accomplish. Burglaries furnish one example for this claim. In the United States, most burglaries are committed when the occupants are not at home or in the immediate vicinity. The reason is that burglars are more frightened of being killed by an occupant than they are of being captured or killed by the police. They understand what many gun control advocates do not: Civilians legally kill far more felons than the police do.

A gun gives a potential victim an option that he or she would not otherwise have except to leave the victim at the mercy of an attacker. It also gives the innocent gun owner peace of mind. A gun offers real security to many people. People who report to the *National Crime Survey* that they defended themselves with a weapon were less likely to lose property in a robbery or be injured in an assault than those who did not defend themselves. It is not surprising, then, that burglars are less likely to enter occupied homes in the United States than they are in Europe, where people are not likely to have guns.

A survey by pollster Peter Hart in 1981 revealed that nine percent of all handgun-owning households had used a handgun for defense in the previous five years. According to a study by Gary Kleck in 1983, up to 2.5 million crimes are prevented each year in the United States by citizens using firearms. In most cases, the potential victim does not fire a shot. A poll published in *USA Today* (December 30, 1993) showed that one in seven (14 percent) of those surveyed had used a gun in self-defense.

The realization by a would-be criminal that a neighborhood is well armed is a deterrent against crime. A number of case studies can be cited to illustrate this point. In Orlando, Florida, in the months between October 1966 and March 1967, the Orlando Police Department trained more than 2,500 women to use guns. The police organized the campaign in response to a big increase in rape in the city. Rape increased from 12.8 per 100,000 citizens in 1965 to 35.9 per 100,000 in 1966. The news media gave much attention to the program. By 1968, Orlando's rape rate declined to 4.1 per 100,000. In 1968, the rape rate in Florida cities other than Orlando increased. Publicized firearms training programs also played a role in reducing armed robberies in Highland Park, Michigan, drugstore robberies in New Orleans, and grocery store robberies in Detroit.

To be sure, accidents happen. Having a gun in a home means that someone may use that gun improperly or accidentally. But gun experts, including the NRA and the Sporting Arms and Ammunition Manufacturer's Institute, agree that safe handling of a firearm requires that guns be stored unloaded in a locked area separate from the ammunition. What is needed, then, is more education about the handling of firearms rather than the banning of firearms.

Substitutes. As indicated above, human beings have been killing other human beings long before guns were ever invented. There is no reason to believe that the banning of handguns would mean that human beings would be any less resourceful today than they were in the pre-gun era.

People intent on killing may rely on knives. They use guns to kill at higher rates than they use knives to kill because guns are more efficient than knives. But this fact does not mean that they could not use knives under different circumstances. Gun control advocates overstate their case when they talk about knives being less dangerous than guns. In their zeal to ban guns, gun control advocates point to the fact that when a gun is used, the chances of a death are about five times as great as when a knife is used. The problem with this fact is that it is often presented in a misleading manner because it implies that guns are five times as deadly as knives. The truth is that people who decide to use guns rather than knives are more intent on killing. Given an absence of guns, people with a strong intention to kill would be just as effective using knives as they are with guns.

Gun control advocates also say that in the absence of guns, criminals would be forced to choose less dangerous weapons. No doubt, if handguns were banned effectively, some criminals would carry knives and clubs. Assuming for the sake of argument that knives and clubs would be less dangerous than handguns (an assumption that is doubtful, to be sure), gun control advocates ignore the fact that a ban on handguns would likely lead to the use of weapons that are generally recognized to be more dangerous, such as sawed-off shotguns and sawed-off rifles. A sawed-off shotgun or rifle could measure anywhere from 7 to 20 inches in length and could as easily be concealed as a handgun. Unless a police officer searched a person, the gun would not be easily observable to a potential victim or law-enforcement official. Long guns, then, could become crime weapons even if handguns were effectively banned. If government drives handguns out of existence, hoodlums will turn to long guns. Many rifles and shotguns are no more expensive than the handguns used in most crimes. And people who are criminals are, by definition, willing to break the law. If they are willing to break the law on robbing and raping, they will be willing to substitute long guns for banned handguns.

Alternatives. Ordinary citizens in many situations need to be armed because they cannot count on the police to protect them. The police themselves say that they are not responsible for individual protection. They contend that their function is to deter crime in general in such matters as responding to emergencies, patrolling, and apprehending suspects after a crime has been committed.

The reluctance of police to assure individual protection can be appreciated given the enormity of their responsibilities and the limitations of their resources. As medical researchers Garen J. Wintemute, Stephen P. Teret, and Jess F. Krause write: "Even if all 500,000 police officers were assigned to patrol, they could not protect 240 million citizens from upwards of 10 million criminals who enjoy the luxury of deciding when or where to strike. But we have nothing like 500,000 patrol officers...." That the police have "no duty to protect individuals" is well established in court proceedings. In 1856, in the case of *South v. Maryland*, the Supreme Court stated this rule. The police have a responsibility to protect the community at large rather than particular individuals.

Publicized firearms training programs may deter crime in certain areas.

Many Americans became acutely aware of the limitations of the police during the Los Angeles riots in 1992. As mentioned before, when the riots began, the police beat a hasty retreat and left innocent citizens to fend for themselves. It is no wonder that some citizens, though respectful of the work of the police, feel that the police are incapable of dealing with the sheer volume of crime in the United States. Some of the more cynical citizens say: "Call for a cop, and call for a pizza. See which comes first." People who are at risk cannot rely on the police. This is particularly true for women who face threats from abusive husbands and boyfriends.

Guns offer effective protection. Alternatives, such as chemical and pepper sprays, self-defense techniques, and personal alarms, can be helpful, but

One of the ways that police officers protect the community at large is by patrolling the streets.

these alternatives have drawbacks. Chemical sprays are not legal in every state and locality. Often, women who buy these sprays are not trained in using them effectively. Women may do more harm to themselves than to assailants under such conditions. In addition, women with chemical sprays may develop a false sense of security and walk in areas that may be dangerous to their safety. Knowledge of self-defense is helpful but impractical for many women either because of time, expense, or health reasons. Personal alarms can be useful but may go off by accident, just as car alarms do from time to time in the middle of the night.

Practical policy. Banning guns to deter crime would be highly impractical. If Gary Kleck is correct that fewer than two percent of handguns are ever involved in crime or if, as some researchers argue, even ten percent of handguns are ever involved in crime, it would be impossible to get the support of the American people to give up their guns. With more than 70 million handguns in circulation, the police would have great trouble in locating the guns. No doubt millions of citizens will follow the law, but the last group of people to accept the law will be the criminals—the very group of people that the law would be designed to disarm.

Moreover, the United States has had experience with banning an item that was in great demand. Banning guns would have the same chance of success as banning alcohol during Prohibition. The Eighteenth Amendment to the Constitution, ratified (approved) in 1919, prohibited the manufacture and sale of alcoholic beverages. But the desire for alcohol led to a widespread disregard for the law, as bootleggers—gangsters who illegally traded in alcohol—satisfied the demand. In 1933, Prohibition was repealed with the ratification (formal legal approval) of the Twenty-First Amendment to the Constitution, and the "noble experiment," as it was called, was ended.

Gun control is also politically impractical because so many law-abiding citizens feel strongly that they need guns for self-protection. Political scientist James Q. Wilson notes in this regard: "The average legislator simply cannot afford to come before his or her constituents with the following proposal: 'Your government, having failed to protect you against crime, now proposes to strip from you what you regard as an effective means of self-defense as well as an enjoyable hobby.'"

The answer to controlling the abuse of firearms is to control criminals, not law-abiding citizens. And here the criminal justice system is at fault. Most people who commit a violent act have committed a violent act before. The best way to reduce gun violence is to go after people with records of violent behavior. Every year 60,000 criminals are convicted of serious crimes and do not go to prison. "We don't have a gun problem in America, we have an enforcement problem," says NRA executive vice president Wayne LaPierre. Only four criminals go to prison for every 100 reported crimes. As Paxton Quigley writes: "For every hundred prisoners with life sentences, twenty-five are freed before their third year; forty-two are out by their seventh year; and people acquitted of murder by reason of insanity spend an average of only five hundred days in mental hospitals before being released."

Firearms violence will decline, moreover, when the police use more effective tactics for dealing with criminals than they have in the past. They should be more aggressive in searching for guns, for example. In 1995, a number of cities were reporting that by heavy frisking of suspects, drug dealers and gang members were leaving their guns at home. Police are also searching for weapons when they stop people for minor violations like public beer drinking and loud radio playing.

By adopting such a policy, New York City reported a drop in murders by handgun there in the first six months of 1995 by 40.7 percent from the first six months of 1994. And by July 16, 1995, New York City police reported 1,714 shooting incidents, 733 fewer than during the same period in the previous year, and 1,962 shooting victims, 818 fewer than the year before.

Guns are not the major problem in crime in America. Criminals are the problem. An effective criminal justice system would go a long way to reducing crime. Until that system is put in place, innocent people need to be allowed to have guns to defend themselves because they cannot always count on the police to do the job.

Chapter 4

GUNS, SUICIDES, AND ACCIDENTS

Debate: Will Gun Control Reduce the Number of Suicides and Accidents?

• A man down on his luck because his wife has left him goes to his desk, removes a handgun from the drawer, loads the gun, and shoots and kills himself.

• A woman told that she is in the early stages of Alzheimer's disease, a severe mental disorder that produces irreversible decay in the ability to think and reason, takes her life with a handgun bullet through her head rather than experience the hardship of a lingering death.

Scenes such as these involving the sad decisions of people who are depressed are not uncommon in many countries. Each year, guns claim more lives from suicides than from homicides in America. In 1991, for example, the police reported 18,526 firearm suicides and 18,350 firearm homicides in the United States.

Guns also play a role in death and injuries as a result of an accidental discharge of a firearm. The police report many incidents in which a person cleaning a gun accidentally fires the weapon, killing the gun owner or some innocent bystander. Similarly, it is not unusual for a police file to contain a report of a child who finds a gun in a closet and mistaking the weapon for a toy accidentally kills or wounds someone, maybe a brother, sister, or friend.

The many incidents of guns in suicides and accidents that occur in the United States have led gun control advocates to argue that one of the benefits of gun control is that it will reduce the number of people who die each year from suicides and accidents. But opponents of gun control deny this claim and say that the number of suicides and accidents could be reduced without gun control.

DEBATED:

WILL GUN CONTROL REDUCE THE NUMBER OF SUICIDES AND ACCIDENTS?

Yes. When Americans think about guns, what first comes to their minds is crime. But guns take a heavy toll of life through suicides and accidents, too. Effective gun control measures would reduce the tragic loss of lives that are taken in this manner.

Suicides. The handgun is an instrument of death and injury in attempted suicide. A person who attempts suicide is more likely to be successful by using a handgun than, say, poison or a knife. In the United States the rate of growth of handgun use for purposes of suicide is increasing more rapidly than for other means.

Guns take more lives in suicides than they do in homicides in the United States. In fact, guns are used far more frequently than knives, which is the second most popular method. The reason why guns are so lethal in suicide attempts is because a person determined to commit suicide looks for an easy way to get the job done, and using a gun seems to be the easiest way. It is fast and decisive. In contrast to some other way of committing suicide, such as taking poison or subjecting oneself to inhaling carbon monoxide (an odorless, poisonous gas), a gun offers little chance for someone to intervene to save the victim from death or from changing his or her mind.

We can get some idea of what the difference in the choice of method in attempted suicide means to the outcome of the suicide attempt when we examine the different suicide patterns between men and women. In attempted suicides, men are likely to use handguns. Women, in contrast, are likely to use pills or some means other than handguns. As Josh Sugarmann observes, handguns are more deadly than other means because "although women try to kill themselves four times as often as men, men succeed three to four times as often." He adds that as women buy handguns, increases are also being seen in their suicide success rates.

On close examination, such a result is not surprising. Often, when people attempt suicide, they do so at a time in their lives when they are emotionally disturbed and are really crying for help. If they choose poison as the instrument of their suicide attempt, it is quite possible that they will be rescued. But because firearms are so lethal, it is unlikely that they can survive a self-inflicted bullet to the head.

Guns take a particularly high toll in the suicides of young people. Suicide is the third leading cause of death among children and adolescents in the United States, a rate that has doubled in the last 30 years, the increase due almost solely to firearms.

Although when most people talk about gun control, they think mostly of the victims of crime, they should recognize that the lowering of crime is but one benefit. A greater benefit of gun control in terms of numbers would be a reduction in the number of suicides.

Accidents. Having concerns about crime, many Americans purchase guns with the expectation that they will be able to use their guns to protect themselves and their loved ones from a criminal intent on robbery or personal assault. Although the goal of security is noble, the reality of security is that the possession of a gun poses a greater threat to the innocent gun owner than it does to a criminal. A gun provides an innocent person with a false sense of security rather than the reality of security.

This difference between the belief in and the reality of security can be best understood by examining how an innocent victim would handle a firearm and then evaluating the consequences of the way that person handles that weapon. An innocent person who buys a gun for protection recognizes that a criminal usually has the advantage of surprise. That is to say that a would-be robber or rapist would enter a home secretly and have a gun at the ready in case of any challenge by a potential victim carrying a gun. For a potential victim of crime to place a gun under lock and key in some hard-to-reach part of the home would mean that the weapon would not be available at the time it is most needed for protection. The best way for an innocent gun owner to be prepared—or at least to have the best chance of avoiding robbery or assault—is to have the gun loaded and placed where it is easy to get at.

A loaded gun in an accessible location, however, is a disaster waiting to happen. Someone coming upon the gun might not think that it is loaded. And a child, thinking that the gun was a toy, might playfully shoot it and kill someone, maybe even himself or herself. In fact, thousands of people are inadvertently killed or wounded in this manner in the United States every year.

In its literature, the NRA mentions the low number of accidental fatalities caused by firearms, but it does not mention how many nonfatal injuries occur from accidental shootings. However, the subject of accidental shooting injuries has been researched by the GAO, which studied ten major police departments that kept records of nonfatal gunshot injuries. It found that out of 532 accidental shootings that occurred in 1988 and 1989, only five had resulted in death. The injury-to-death ratio, therefore, was 105 to 1.

The GAO indicated that one could not provide a national figure because many police departments do not collect this kind of information. But as writer Erik Larson notes in his book *Lethal Passage: How the Travels of a Single Handgun Expose the Roots of America's Gun Crisis* that if the 105-to-1 ratio were accurate, then "157,600 accidental, nonfatal gunshot injuries occur each year." If Larson is correct, then the number of accidental, nonfatal gunshot injuries in the United States is equal to the number of people who live in a small American city about the size of Chattanooga, Tennessee, or Fort Lauderdale, Florida. That figure is not trivial.

Particularly noteworthy is the nature of the victims of firearm accidents. Franklin E. Zimring, head of the Earl Warren Legal Institute of the University of California, Berkeley, notes: "The population groups that have the highest fatality rates for [firearm] accidents are male children and adolescents, who are generally inexperienced in using guns and are often tempted to play with them. Clearly, if young people did not have access to guns, the death rate would drop."

Arthur L. Kellerman and Donald T. Reay conducted research that bears on the subject of guns and accidents. (Kellerman is an associate professor of medicine at the University of Tennessee in Memphis. Reay is chief medical examiner at the King County Medical Examiner's Office in Seattle, Washington.) They studied all gunshot deaths that occurred in King County, Washington (which includes Seattle and Bellevue).

Their research emphasis was in gunshot deaths that occurred in the house where the firearm involved was kept. They found that guns kept in King County homes were involved in the deaths of friends or acquaintances 12 times as often as in those of strangers. They write: "For every time a gun in

A loaded gun left in an accessible location could be a disaster waiting to happen.

the home was involved in a 'self-protection' homicide, we noted 1.3 accidental gunshot deaths, 4.6 criminal homicides, and 37 firearm-related suicides."

It is clear that the possession of a gun in the home is a greater danger to someone in the household or a guest than it is to an intruder. Gun control policy that takes guns out of the home will make private citizens more secure rather than less secure.

NO. However dreadful suicides and firearm accidents are, gun control is not the solution for them. A sane approach to preventing suicides and firearm accidents must be based on an effective alternative to gun control.

Suicides. Suicides are tragic events, not only because of the lives lost in such deaths but also because of the toll they take on the minds and hearts of the loved ones left behind. But people have been committing suicide long before the invention of firearms, and we would be foolish to think that a country with a strong gun control policy would effectively reduce the number of suicides.

People who commit suicide with a gun may be determined to kill themselves, and a gun is only one convenient means for a suicidal person to accomplish his or her mission. In the absence of guns, suicidal people may choose knives, poison, or carbon monoxide to take their lives. They can jump off bridges or buildings. If a person is serious about suicide, he or she will usually try the most lethal means of achieving that goal available to him or her.

Guns are the instrument of suicide but not the cause. People who commit suicide do so for such reasons as depression, economic or other personal failures, poor health, alcoholism, and drug abuse. Some may use a gun to end the effort of coping with their problems, but the key element is not the gun but rather the failure to find help to solve their problems.

Because the pattern of suicides varies from country to country, we can study the possible connection of gun ownership to suicides by looking not only at suicide in the United States but at suicide in other countries, as well. Japan, Great Britain, and Canada are countries where firearms are difficult to acquire, and Switzerland is a country in which many people have firearms.

The Japanese gun suicide rate is one-fiftieth that of the United States. But the overall Japanese suicide rate is nearly twice as high as America's. Teenage suicide is 30 percent more frequent in Japan than in the United States. As far as suicides are concerned, the Japanese people who commit suicide follow a long tradition of using a knife rather than a gun.

The percentage of suicides by gun in Great Britain is down since 1890, but the suicide rate has remained constant. The suicide rate is about the same as it was at the turn of the century, although in the period from 1890 to the present Great Britain moved from a legal system of no gun control to one of strict gun control.

The suicide rate is high in Switzerland. In fact, it is more than double that of the United States. But the percentage of suicides committed with guns is relatively low in that country. Switzerland is a country in which many households have firearms. The suicide rate in the United States is slightly less than in Canada, although Canada possesses fewer guns per person than the United States.

It is true that many countries have high gun use in suicides, but that fact does not mean that if guns are banned, there will be fewer suicides, as the case of Japan illustrates. As David Kopel notes: "Countries with many guns may have more gun-related suicides for the same reason that countries on the ocean have relatively more drowning-related suicides—the availability of a suicide instrument (firearms or water) to which some cultural importance is attached."

To say that guns are responsible for the high number of suicides in the United States is to confuse cause and effect. Finding a solution to suicide requires an understanding of the real psychological, social, and economic problems that produce a feeling of hopelessness and despair.

Accidents. An accident resulting in the death or injury of an innocent person is always a sad event, whether the accident involves drowning, automobile crash, or accidental discharge of a firearm. But the risk of an accidental death from having a gun in one's home is quite small.

If one gets information from television and newspapers, one would believe that accidental shootings take many lives. But the statistics tell otherwise. Here is a list of the top ten causes of death by unintended injuries in 1993 in the United States, ranked from most deaths to least deaths, as provided by the National Safety Council, a public interest group that promotes safety.

As the figures show, automobile accidents cause the most deaths. And falls; poisoning by solids and liquids; drowning; fires, burns, and deaths associated with fires; and suffocation by ingested object cause even more deaths

Motor-vehicle accidents	**42,000**
Falls	**13,500**
Poisoning by solids and liquids	**6,500**
Drowning	**4,800**
Fires, burns, and deaths associated with fires	**4,000**
Suffocation by ingested (swallowed) object	**2,900**
Firearms	**1,600**
Poisoning by gases and vapors	**700**
All other types	**14,000**

than accidents from firearms. But nobody argues that we should ban automobiles because some people die in them. And it would be silly for anyone to argue that we should ban ladders because some people fall off of them and die. What we would say is that people who drive should conduct themselves in a safe manner, as should people who climb ladders.

The same comment could be made of people who own guns. They need to be educated in the safe use and care of firearms. The facts show that Americans are becoming increasingly safety conscious about firearms. According to the National Safety Council, in the period from 1983 to 1993, accidental deaths caused by firearms in the United States decreased from 1,695 to 1,600—a decline of six percent.

The conclusion is that the risk of an accidental death from a firearm has been exaggerated by the advocates of gun control. It is easy to get news media attention when a tragic event such as an accidental death from a firearm occurs. But public policy ought to be shaped by reason rather than emotion if the goal of public policy is to provide the best laws to protect and serve the American people. It would be wrong to dismiss concern for death or injury from firearms. Firearms obviously can discharge accidentally. The solution to reducing the number of accidents is in tough safety training—not banning handguns.

One step toward reducing the number of accidental deaths caused by firearms is educating gun owners about safe use and care of them.

The kind of people who commit many gun accidents are people who are alcoholics, have records of drunken driving, and have previous arrests for assault. Most gun accidents do not involve children, although gun accidents that do involve children receive much publicity. Of the 1,600 accidental firearms deaths in 1993, only 220 involved people 14 years old or younger. The breakdown by age is as follows:

Age	0-4	5-14	15-24	25-44	45-64	65-74	75 & Over
Deaths	40	180	550	450	210	60	110

Gary Kleck puts the accidental deaths of children by firearms in perspective. He shows that claiming that accidents from guns are the fourth or fifth highest cause of accidents to young people is misleading. He writes: "Only the first of the leading accidental causes, motor vehicle accidents, is responsible for a large number of child deaths. Out of more than 20,000 deaths, from all causes, of children age 1 to 14 in 1987, over 4,000 were due to motor vehicle accidents, compared to about 250 due to gun accidents (National Safety Council 1989)."

Guns are used by honest and law-abiding citizens for many legitimate purposes, such as hunting and personal and family security. It is wrong to tell these people that they are in more danger from having guns than from having no guns. Arguments that gun possession is dangerous because of possible suicide or accidents undermine the safety of people and ignore the measures that people can take to avoid those situations.

Chapter 5
GUNS AND THE CONSTITUTION

Debate: Do the American People Have a Collective, Rather than an Individual, Right to Bear Arms?

The entrance to the former headquarters of the NRA building in Washington, D.C., displayed these words:

> The right of the people to keep and bear arms shall not be infringed.

These are words from the Second Amendment to the Constitution of the United States, the document that describes the powers and institutions of the U.S. government. The words at the NRA entrance are not the complete text of the Second Amendment but are, rather, only the words from the second part of the text. The first part of that amendment reads:

> A well regulated Militia, being necessary to the security of a free State...

The failure by the NRA to include the full text of the Second Amendment tells much about the controversy between the supporters and opponents of gun control. For if the Constitution grants an individual right of the people to bear (carry) arms, people may have arms for their own self-protection. This "individual rights" view of the Second Amendment supports the position of opponents of gun control. Because the Constitution is the supreme law of the land, they argue, any law in conflict with that document is by definition unconstitutional and cannot be binding, whether the law deals with gun control or any other matter.

If, however, the Constitution grants a collective (group) right to bear arms, citizens may possess arms only to defend the state. This "collective rights" view of the Second Amendment supports the position of advocates of gun control. They argue that individuals have a right to bear arms to serve the state governments in forming a militia (defined in Chapter 1 as an armed force of citizen soldiers who may be called to service during emergencies). According to this line of thinking, Congress has the constitutional authority to pass laws regulating an individual's possession of firearms so long as it does not deny the states the right to form militias.

A consideration of the issues involved in interpreting the Second Amendment requires some basic background information. Specifically, an explanation of the meaning of a militia, the historical background of the Constitution and the Bill of Rights, and the authority and decisions of the Supreme Court is necessary in order to make an informed judgment about the meaning of the Second Amendment. A militia and a standing army are two forms of military organization in American history. In contrast to a militia, a standing army is a military organization made up of regular forces (either volunteers or draftees) that are in continuing military service for a fixed period of time. Although we refer to militias as citizen soldiers, a more precise distinction is

Militia men, as they appeared in 18th-century America.

general militia and a select militia. A general militia refers to the entire body of citizens. A select militia means a smaller segment of citizens who commit themselves to military duty during times of emergency.

When the United States was under British colonial rule, the militia was the military organization of the settlers. During times in which the settlers were in danger from attack by Native Americans or foreign powers, the male settlers had an obligation to serve in militias. In so serving, they furnished their own uniforms and weapons. When the emergency was over, the men returned to civilian life.

It was not until the American Revolutionary War that the former colonies, now known as the United States, formed a regular army. George Washington, commander of the Continental Army, relied on both the militia and a regular army to fight the war.

After the British were defeated in the war, the colonists established a weak central government under what was called the Articles of Confederation. In that system, state governments had superior powers to the central government. Congress, which was the legislative (lawmaking) institution, had only limited powers. Under the Articles of Confederation, the government proved ineffective in dealing with economic, political, and foreign policy problems.

Many political leaders agreed that the Articles needed to be changed and that a stronger central government had to be formed. A group of political leaders met in Philadelphia in 1787 and produced what is known as the Constitution of the United States. These leaders came from all of the 13 states that made up the United States at that time. The debates at the Constitutional Convention revealed differing views about many issues. Some of the most important differences were over the proper role of government in society, the ability of a people to secure their freedom against an oppressive government, the relationship between the branches of the national government (Congress, the President, and the courts), and the character of a federal system (in which powers are divided or shared between the central, or federal, government, and the states).

The political leaders (known in American history as the Founders, or Framers of the Constitution) showed great interest in the organization and structure of the armed forces. The Constitution as finally written expressed that interest in many ways. Specifically for military matters, the Constitution provided for two kinds of military organizations—a regular armed force and a militia.

Under Article I, section 8, of the Constitution, Congress has the power to "raise and support armies" and "provide and maintain a Navy." Congress can "provide for calling forth the Militia" in order "to execute the Laws of the Union, suppress Insurrections and repel Invasions." Congress can also "provide for organizing, arming, and disciplining, the Militia, and for governing such Part of them as may be employed in the Service of the United States."

But the states retain power over the militias. Specifically, the Constitution reserves "to the States respectively, the Appointment of the Officers, and the Authority of training the Militia according to the discipline prescribed by Congress." And the President serves as commander in chief of the armed forces, including the militia.

Once the Founders had completed their work, they submitted their proposed Constitution to the states for approval. Many people in the states feared that the Constitution as drawn up in Philadelphia did not provide enough protection to citizens against the power of the federal government. These people called for changes in the form of amendments to the Constitution that would guarantee individual rights.

Some of the Founders argued that including these rights would be unnecessary because the Constitution, as written, would protect individual rights. Besides, they said, states could assure those rights in their own state constitutions. But to get the necessary approval for the Constitution, the document's supporters agreed to add amendments. When the first Congress met, it proposed amendments to the Constitution, and the ten amendments that were adopted by Congress and ratified by the states became known as the Bill of Rights. These rights cover many areas, including freedom of speech, the press, and religion; rights of a person in criminal proceedings; and rights dealing with protection against unreasonable searches. As mentioned earlier, the Second Amendment deals with the right to bear arms.

Since the adoption of the Constitution and the Bill of Rights, federal, state, and local governments have passed laws regulating the sale, ownership, carrying, and use of firearms. In all, these governments have passed more than 20,000 laws dealing with firearms. Nonetheless, the constitutional issue of the meaning of the Second Amendment remains a subject of continuing controversy in the American political system.

In this system, the Supreme Court as the highest court in the nation decides cases dealing with disputes about the Constitution. Although the Supreme Court has heard a number of cases involving gun control, it has never decided directly about whether the right to bear arms is an individual or collective right. In fact, the Supreme Court has had very little to say about interpreting the Second Amendment. In contrast, lower courts at the federal or state level have made many decisions interpreting the amendment.

The issue about the meaning of the amendment has practical policy consequences that can affect the right of citizens to buy, own, carry, and use guns. If the Supreme Court decides that the Second Amendment gives an individual a right to bear arms, then opponents of gun control will have a strong legal basis for opposing gun control laws on constitutional grounds.

Such an interpretation would not necessarily strike down all gun control laws, however. Legal scholars note in this regard that although the First Amendment states that Congress may make no law abridging (limiting) freedom of speech, Congress has passed laws that abridge speech. And the Supreme Court has upheld the constitutionality of some of these laws. For example, the Sedition Law of 1918, enacted in World War I when the United States was at war against Germany, made certain kinds of speech illegal. The law specifically made unlawful any "word or act [favoring] the cause of

the German empire... or [opposing] the cause of the United States."
(Sedition is conduct or language that encourages rebellion against
the authority of a country.)

A Supreme Court interpretation approving the individual rights
approach to the Second Amendment, however, would damage
the prospects for effective gun control legislation. Advocates of gun
control could attempt to get around the Court's decision by
amending the Constitution in a manner that in effect strikes down
the Second Amendment or rewrites it to clarify its meaning as a
collective right. Amending the Constitution would be a difficult
process, however, because to do so would require approval by
two-thirds of the members of each chamber of Congress—the
House of Representatives and the Senate—and ratification by three-
fourths of the state legislatures. In the more than 200 years since the
Constitution was adopted, it has been amended only 26 times (with
the first ten coming into force in the first Congress). So the Supreme
Court interpretation of the Second Amendment still can have a
profound impact on gun control policy today.

DEBATED:

DO THE AMERICAN PEOPLE HAVE A COLLECTIVE, RATHER THAN AN INDIVIDUAL, RIGHT TO BEAR ARMS?

Yes. In writing about the NRA's interpretation of the Second Amendment, which asserts an individual rather than a collective right, the late Chief Justice of the Supreme Court Warren Burger described it as "one of the greatest pieces of fraud, I repeat the word fraud, on the American public by special interest groups that I have ever seen in my lifetime...." A study of the origins and history of the Second Amendment supports Burger's view that the purpose of the Second Amendment was to guarantee that the right of states to form militias should not be denied. The collective rights interpretation is based on the legacy of English history to the American legal system, the militia in 18th-century America, the Constitution of the United States, and the changing character of warfare.

English history. The Second Amendment, like much of the American legal system, owes its origins to the English experience because the colonies were established by England. The men who wrote the Constitution were influenced specifically by developments in English common law—the system of law based on custom and precedent (a court decision that is used as a standard to decide similar cases) and by the great works of legal writers.

Even before the Norman Conquest of England in 1066, England relied on a militia rather than a standing army for maintaining order and providing military security from foreign enemies. Kings understood that militias were less costly to finance than were permanent armies.

People had police responsibilities, too. According to the common law, citizens were required to pursue criminals and were subject to fine and imprisonment

The control of the militia was one cause of the English Civil War.

if they did not join a posse—a group of people organized by a public official to assist in law enforcement—for this purpose. Such a system of law enforcement was necessary because there was no professional police force. It was not until the 19th century that England had a professional police force. To perform the military and criminal justice duties, citizens were expected to furnish their own weapons and be able to use them.

Englishmen had a duty to serve in the militia, which could be used only for purposes of defense and could not be taken out of the country. Because citizen soldiers were needed for military service, they were required to have weapons and know how to use them.

Although Englishmen had a duty to possess arms, government has been regulating that use for hundreds of years. In 1328, for example, the Statute of Northampton provided that no man should "go nor ride armed by night or by day, in Fairs, Markets, nor in the presence of Justices or other Ministers, nor in no part elsewhere." In 1671, the Game Act restricted the class of persons who could possess guns to noblemen and those who owned lands worth 100 pounds. Even the English Bill of Rights (1689) provided that Protestants could have arms for their defense "suitable to their Conditions and as allowed by Law." And in the centuries following the English Bill of Rights, Great Britain passed many laws restricting the right to possess arms.

The history of 17th-century England is particularly important in understanding the right to bear arms. A struggle between the monarchy and Parliament (the legislative body) led to civil war in the country between 1642 and 1648. The victory of Parliament resulted in the execution of the king, Charles I, in 1649 and the abolition of the monarchy. After a period in which a dictatorship was established under Oliver Cromwell, the monarchy was restored in 1660 when Charles II became king.

In 1685, James II, a Roman Catholic, succeeded to the throne. He attempted to fill important positions with Roman Catholics, a move that made him unpopular in a mostly Protestant country. During the period of James II's rule, moreover, Protestants were disarmed but Catholics were permitted to have arms.

In the Glorious Revolution of 1688, James II fled to France and William of Orange became king, ruling jointly with his wife, Mary I. In coming to the throne, William and Mary accepted a Declaration of Rights assuring dominance of Parliament over royal power. Parliament enacted the Declaration of Rights as the English Bill of Rights in 1689.

Nowhere in that document is it written that all Englishmen have a right to bear arms. Instead, the right is granted to one group of Englishmen—Protestants. In the words of the English Bill of Rights, Protestants "may have arms for their defence." But even here, it is clear that such use is limited for Protestants only as "suitable to their Conditions and as allowed by Law." In other words, in one of the most important documents in the history of liberty, government has the authority to regulate the possession of arms. The English Bill of Rights, then, is not a statement assuring Englishmen that they have an unlimited right to bear arms.

Critics of the collective rights view often point to the eminent legal authority William Blackstone, whose legal writings became the great authority of English common law in England and the United States. It is true that in his work Blackstone

William Blackstone (1723–1780)

mentioned the right to bear arms. But he did not list the right to bear arms as one of the three great and primary rights of personal security, personal liberty, and private property. Instead, he referred to the right to bear arms as an auxiliary (supporting) right. And this right, said Blackstone, is limited by "having arms for their defense, suitable to their condition and degree and such as allowed by law."

Those who turn to English history to prove an individual right to bear arms fail to take into account that the right is not absolute. For English history recognizes limitations of that right and relates the right to the needs of the country.

The militia in 18th-century America. To understand the meaning of the Second Amendment, one must recognize the significance of the militia in early American history. Like the English for most of its history, Americans relied on the militia rather than a standing army for their defense.

The settlers who experienced hardships in surviving in the colonies did not have the income to support a standing army. In addition, they had a loathing for a standing army, which they regarded as a threat to liberty. Their hostility to a standing army developed in part from their experience with a standing army that England used to maintain order in the American colonies. Among the hated practices of these soldiers was the requirement that English troops be quartered (housed) by the colonists. Since those troops often consisted of men who were unruly, it is no wonder that the colonists resented and feared them.

In the 18th century, all of the colonies had militias. And the independent states that replaced the colonies continued to have militias during and after the Revolutionary War. Adult white males had a legal responsibility in the states to become militia members. Although the American rebels established a regular army during the Revolutionary War, the new nation reduced the number of men in that army to only a few hundred once the war had ended. The American people continued to prefer to rely on the militia, which they trusted, rather than on a standing army, which they feared.

In the late 18th century, then, Americans relied principally on militias for their defense. The militias were organized by the states, which could arm them and direct them for the purpose of enforcing the law, fighting a foreign power, or stopping a rebellion.

The Constitution. Once the colonies became independent states, they wrote their own constitutions. These state constitutions differed from state to state in the way that they declared fundamental principles and provided for organizing government. But they recognized in one way or another the importance of the militia in a free society. Americans believed that the militia would provide for military security and police power. They thought, too, that it would protect liberty in case of domestic unrest and prevent an individual or group from gathering so much armed power as to establish a tyranny (dictatorship).

The state constitutions, which describe the fundamental laws and principles about the nature and functions of state governments, dealt in different ways with the right to bear arms and to organize the militia. But most state constitutions provided that individuals should have a right to bear arms only for service in the militia. Only four states had a specific provision in their constitutions listing a right to bear arms. And the Virginia Declaration of Rights, which was adopted as part of the Virginia Constitution of 1776, makes no mention of a right to bear arms. The text of Article 13 of the Virginia Constitution states:

> That a well-regulated Militia, composed of the body of the people, trained to arms, is the proper, natural and safe defence of a free State; that Standing Armies, in time of peace, should be avoided as dangerous to liberty; and that, in all cases, the military should be under strict subordination to and governed by the civil power.

An understanding of state constitutions requires close attention to how specific words were used. In this regard, historian Lawrence Delbert Cress correctly notes that state constitutions regularly used the words "man" or "person" with respect to "individual rights, such as freedom of conscience." But the term "the people" in the constitutions refers to the "sovereign [self-governing] citizenry" organized as a group.

The men who wrote the Constitution of the United States had many of the same thoughts as the men who wrote the state constitutions. They understood the dangers that the new nation faced, particularly the idea that the nation would need to have a military force strong enough to serve security interests but not so powerful as to destroy liberty. The Constitution provided for a regular army to be controlled by the federal government and for a militia with power largely in the hands of the states.

When the Framers wrote the Second Amendment, they did not see it as giving the private citizen a right to have arms for his or her own sake. Rather, the purpose of the amendment was to assure that citizens would have a right to be armed so that they could become part of a militia. That is why the first part of the Second Amendment presents a governing purpose for the meaning of the amendment, namely "a well regulated Militia being necessary to the security of a free State."

In interpreting the Constitution, the Supreme Court has never declared any gun control law to be unconstitutional because it was in conflict with the Second Amendment. The Supreme Court has directly ruled on Second Amendment issues only in four cases: *United States v. Cruikshank* (1876), *Presser v. Illinois* (1886), *Miller v. Texas* (1894), and *United States v. Miller* (1939). It is clear from these cases that the Court interprets the Second Amendment as a collective right, which holds that the states have a right to maintain militias. Lower federal court and state court decisions support the collective rights approach to the Second Amendment.

Irrelevance of the Second Amendment. A Constitution is a living document and needs to be interpreted in terms of changing conditions. In the 18th century, this nation could rely heavily on a militia and could draw upon the well-armed citizenry to furnish the troops and weapons to meet a national need. But as early as the American Revolution, it became obvious that a regular armed force was needed. George Washington, among many leaders, recognized the weaknesses of relying on the militia during the Revolutionary War. And in the years following the Revolution, those concerned with national security put emphasis upon strengthening the regular armed forces.

The changing nature of technology in the 20th century has transformed the very idea of the right to bear arms. In the 18th century, the possession of small arms (handheld firearms) was important both as a means of security for a community and as a check on tyranny. At that time, people who owned personal firearms were likely to have a single shot musket or pistol. Such weapons were similar to the weapons used for military purposes. Although heavier weapons were available in private hands, battles were fought by infantry or cavalry with weapons similar to those used by civilians in hunting or for personal protection.

But weaponry today is far more powerful than existed in the 18th century. Semiautomatic weapons, for example, have considerably more firepower than the old Revolutionary War weapons. Because of the changing character of weaponry, the case for widespread availability of firearms has changed. There is much truth to the comment of David E. Petzal, who writes the "Endangered Tradition" column in *Field and Stream* magazine. He writes: "When the Bill of Rights was framed, the average farmer had the same weapon, the smoothbore musket, as soldiers." But today, Petzal notes, "An Uzi or an AKM or an AK-47 should be no more generally available than a Claymore mine or a block of C4 explosive."

Also, today we have professional police departments whose members are trained to use guns and to enforce the law. No longer do we require ordinary citizens to form posses to deal with criminal matters. The need for private citizens to possess arms for military and police purposes is outmoded.

It is clear from historical research that the American people never had an individual right to bear arms, as the NRA would have us believe. Gun control legislation can be enacted without fear that we are trampling upon the Bill of Rights. We need to interpret the Second Amendment to fit the changing times.

No. People who argue that the Constitution confers a collective,

rather than an individual, right to bear arms ignore the historical evidence in offering their interpretation. They are more interested in getting gun control laws enacted than in understanding legitimate constitutional principles. For the individual rights view is supported by an understanding of English history, militias in the 18th century, the Constitution, and the relevance of the Second Amendment, even under conditions of modern technology.

English history. Until the 17th century, the possession of arms in England was a duty that Englishmen were required to follow in service to the militia. But developments in that century turned what had been a duty for military service and law enforcement into a right to bear arms.

During the 17th century, efforts were made to take arms away from many Englishmen. Parliament passed the Game Act of 1671 requiring hunters to own property and preventing anyone who was not a property owner from owning hunting equipment. For the first time, the act took away from the majority of Englishmen their legal right to keep weapons. The aristocracy and the wealthy middle class, thus, had almost exclusive power to control weapons. After 1680, King Charles II used the Militia Act of 1662 to disarm his opponents. And James II, who succeeded Charles II, relied on the Militia Act and the Game Act to disarm his Protestant subjects.

Englishmen recognized that they needed to guarantee their right to own weapons. The outrage they felt achieved legal recognition in 1689 when Parliament enacted the English Bill of Rights, which condemned the practices of James II. The English Bill of Rights provided "that the Subjects which are Protestants may have Arms for their Defence suitable to their Conditions and as allowed by Law."

Critics of the individual rights view of the Second Amendment argue that the English Bill of Rights was a collective right rather than an individual right.

In this regard, they say that the right to bear arms was applied only to one group (Protestants) and only for collective purposes, such as national defense. But Catholics constituted only two percent of the population in England, so the limitation to Protestants was of little practical significance. Besides, an act of 1689, which became law after the English Bill of Rights was adopted, allowed Catholics to keep all arms needed for self-defense.

Critics of the individual rights view are entirely wrong to cite the English Bill of Rights for their case. The English Bill of Rights makes no mention of the militia. The debates at the convention considering the matter of arms possession show clearly that the English right to have arms is an individual right. The phrase "as allowed by Law," moreover, limited the kind of weapon that could be legally owned to a full-length firearm and made some other modifications. However, none of these modifications limited the right of Englishmen to bear arms.

Many authorities have recognized the importance of the right to bear arms as an individual right. William Blackstone is a case in point. He noted the importance of the individual right to bear arms as a check on tyranny. After listing the rights of Englishmen in the first chapter of his *Commentaries on the Laws of England*, he mentions five auxiliary rights needed to protect and maintain the three great and primary rights of personal security, personal liberty, and private property: "The fifth and last auxiliary right of the subject, that I shall at present mention, is that of having arms for their defence, suitable to their condition and degree, and such as are allowed by law... and is, indeed, a publick allowance under due restrictions, of the natural right of resistance and self preservation, when the sanctions of society and laws are found insufficient to restrain the violence of oppression."

English common law was in the minds of the Framers of the Constitution. And as historian Joyce Lee Malcolm observes of the individual right to be armed: "It was this heritage that Englishmen took with them to the American colonies and this heritage which Americans fought to protect in 1775."

The militia in the 18th century. In colonial times, the militia consisted of the entire adult male citizenry. The age qualification varied among colonies from 15, 16, or 18 to 45, 50, or 60. Most citizens had firearms of one sort or another. Colonial law went beyond English law by requiring citizens to be armed. The harsh conditions of frontier life made possession of arms a necessity for self-defense. Not only did the settlers have to provide for their own defense, but they also had to serve as a sort of police to track down criminals. A professional police force did not appear until the 19th century. Citizens were expected to have their own arms to enforce the law. Even people who were not eligible for militia service, such as the elderly and

Even in the 19th century, lawmen had to form armed groups of citizens, or posses, to track down criminals in some parts of the United States.

seamen who were exempt from militia service, were required by law to keep arms in their households.

In 1792, Congress passed the Militia Act, which defined the militia to include all able-bodied adult male citizens in the United States and required each of them to own a firearm. It is clear that Congress understood the militia to be considered in a broad sense rather than as a formal military force separate from the people.

The Constitution. The men who played such an important role in the struggle for independence and the building of the new nation believed in the wide ownership of arms by the citizenry. They also had fundamental faith in the militia in providing for the military needs of the new nation. They established a constitutional system that sought to achieve both goals. In fact, they held the view that the right to bear arms was inseparable from the right to form a militia.

After the colonists declared independence, they wrote their own state consti-tutions. Many of these constitutions contained their own bills of rights. According to historian Joyce Lee Malcolm: "Those that took this precaution [to write a bill of rights] were careful to indicate their preference for a mili-tia over a standing army and either specifically stated that the people had a right to be armed, or made it necessary by insisting upon a citizen militia that was a general, not a select, militia." So enduring is the commitment to individual self-defense that even today, 31 states have constitutional provi-sions that can be read to guarantee an individual right to bear arms.

The men who wrote the Second Amendment were influenced by the state constitutions, which in a variety of ways expressed the dominant thinking of the times, in opposition to a standing army, in support of a militia, and in favor of an individual's right to bear arms. At times, the right to bear arms was asserted boldly, and at other times, it was related to the establishment of a militia. Pennsylvania's constitution presented these themes in one arti-cle: "That the people have a right to bear arms for the defence of them-selves and the state; and as standing armies in the time of peace are dan-gerous to liberty, they ought not to be kept up; And that the military should be kept under strict subordination to, and governed by, the civil power." As historian Robert E. Stalhope observes: "It is apparent... that Americans of the Revolutionary generation distinguished between the individual's right to keep arms and the need for a militia in which to bear them. Yet it is equally clear that more often than not they considered these rights inseparable."

George Mason said: "To disarm the people [is] the best and most effectual way to enslave them." In 1776, Mason wrote the Virginia Declaration of Rights, which became the model for declarations of rights of the other American colonies under British rule. The Virginia Declaration of Rights includes the provision "that a well regulated Militia, composed of the body of the People, trained to Arms, is the proper, natural, and safe Defence of a free State...." Mason had a clear notion of the nature of the militia. He said: "Who are the Militia? They consist now of the whole people."

In his first draft of the Virginia Constitution of 1776, Thomas Jefferson echoed the view of Mason in his support of the right to bear arms. Jefferson wrote: "No freeman shall be debarred the use of arms in his own lands."

Samuel Adams, governor of Massachusetts and a close friend of Thomas Jefferson, offered an amendment to the Massachusetts convention consider-ing the ratification of the Constitution of the United States: "And that the said Constitution be never construed to authorize Congress to infringe the just lib-erty of the press or the rights of conscience; or to prevent the people of the United States who are peaceable citizens, from keeping their own arms...."

Both opponents and supporters of ratifying the Constitution of the United States recognized the importance of an armed citizenry in preserving liberty. Richard Henry Lee of Virginia, who opposed ratification of the Constitution, considered it "essential that the whole body of the people always possess arms, and be taught alike, especially when young how to use them."

Writing in support of ratification of the Constitution, Alexander Hamilton and James Madison both noted the importance of an armed citizenry in what came to be known as The Federalist Papers. Hamilton wrote in *Federalist* No. 29:

Alexander Hamilton (1757–1804)

Little more can reasonably be aimed at with respect to the people at large than to have them properly armed and equipped....

This will not only lessen the call for military establishments, but if circumstances at any time oblige the government to form an army of any magnitude that army can never be formidable to the liberties of the people while there is a large body of citizens, little if at all inferior to them in discipline and the use of arms, who stand ready to defend their rights and those of their fellow citizens.

Writing in *Federalist* No. 46, James Madison pointed out "the advantage of being armed, which the Americans possess over the people of almost every other nation." And he added: "Notwithstanding the military establishments in the several kingdoms of Europe, which are carried as far as the public resources will bear, the governments are afraid to trust the people with arms." According to

James Madison (1751–1836)

Madison, if the people were armed and organized into militias, "the throne of every tyranny in Europe would be speedily overturned in spite of the legions which surround it."

When the Framers spoke of the militia, they never had in mind a select militia. It was a general militia. In fact, they identified a select militia with a standing army for which they had contempt. Supporters of the collective rights view are wrong to think of the militia as a select militia. In the 18th century, the term militia was rarely used to refer to organized military units. It referred mostly to all citizens qualified for military service (in other words, most adult males).

In 1787, at the time that the Constitutional Convention was formed in Philadelphia, most Americans had firearms, which they needed for hunting and for wars against the Native Americans. The Framers of the Constitution assumed that the people would be armed, and they had no intention of disarming them. That is why there was so little discussion of the subject at the convention.

The case for the individual rights view of the Second Amendment is strengthened by examining the text of the amendment and of the rest of the Bill of Rights. The very context of the Second Amendment shows that the amendment confers an individual right to bear arms. The first four amendments are grouped as individual rights—(First Amendment—right of free speech; Second Amendment—right to bear arms; Third Amendment—no soldier should be quartered in time of peace; and Fourth Amendment—protection to be secure in their persons against unreasonable searches and seizures).

Another way of looking at the Bill of Rights is to examine how the term "the people" is used. In addition to appearing in the Second Amendment, the term "the people" is found in the First, Fourth, Ninth, and Tenth amendments. It is clear that in amendments other than the Second, the term people does not have a collective meaning. Why, then, should the Second Amendment be the only one with a meaning of "the people" defined as "collective"? The answer is that the collective rights view that believes in this meaning is false.

Individual rights supporters misunderstand the meaning of "well-regulated" in the Second Amendment. The term well-regulated militia meant that the Framers of the Constitution assumed that the militia could be organized in some way, such as being organized into formal military units or as being composed of individuals with some knowledge of warfare. But the Framers assumed that the men would have arms and would be trained to use them.

The interpretation of the Second Amendment as providing individual rights was made by some of the most noted judges and lawyers who wrote in the years following the adoption of the Constitution and Bill of Rights. For example, in his *Commentaries on the Constitution* (1833), Joseph Story, an associate justice of the Supreme Court whose legal writings had a great impact on American law, described the militia as "the natural defence of a free country" not only "against sudden foreign invasions" and "domestic insurrections," but also against "domestic usurpations [wrongful or illegal seizures] of power by rulers." Story added that the right of the citizens to keep and bear arms has justly been considered "as the palladium [safeguard] of the liberties of a republic; since it offers a strong moral check against the usurpation and arbitrary power of rulers; and will generally, even if these are successful in the first instance, enable the people to resist and triumph over them."

Although the Supreme Court has considered only a few cases involving the Second Amendment, it is clear that it recognizes the constitutional right of the people to bear arms. None of the decisions in these cases denies the right of the people to own guns.

Relevance of the Second Amendment. Critics of the Second Amendment refer to it as obsolete (no longer useful) because a people armed with small weapons is no match for a modern army with a vast arsenal of weapons or of weapons carrying nuclear warheads across thousands of miles. But such an observation, while correct in noting that technology has changed the nature of warfare, is irrelevant to some of the most significant military events of the 20th century.

There are many examples in the 20th century showing the importance of an armed citizenry. For example, the Soviet Union invaded Afghanistan in 1979 and sought to occupy that remote and developing nation. Yet Afghan guerrilla fighters fought fiercely, and within a few years, the Soviets recognized that they could not succeed and withdrew from the country. The United States, too, had superior weaponry that it used in Vietnam between 1965 and 1974. But the most advanced technology did not prevent a U.S. withdrawal from Vietnam and a victory of the Communist forces. Moreover, many of the postwar anticolonial wars fought in Africa and Asia against European powers resulted in defeat or withdrawal by the technologically superior European armies. Small arms in the hands of the masses of people, then, are still an important military resource that can be used effectively to achieve a political goal.

The American people well understand the constitutional basis of the right to possess arms. This understanding is clear from public opinion polls. For example, a *U.S. News & World Report* poll in 1995 shows that 75 percent of all American voters believe that the Constitution guarantees them the right to own a gun. The specific question was:

Do you agree that the Constitution guarantees you the right to own a gun?

Agree: 75 %

Disagree: 18 %

The case against the individual rights approach to the Second Amendment is currently falling on deaf ears.

Chapter 6
GUNS AND POLITICS

Debate: Is the NRA's Reputation as a Politically Powerful Organization Exaggerated?

In an effort to influence public policy on the manufacture, sale, and use of guns in the United States, private organizations participate actively in the political process. Both supporters and opponents of gun control have either organized new groups or mobilized existing groups to gain the support of public officials and of public opinion, as well. Because government is the organization that has the legal authority to make binding rules on a community, interest groups are particularly alert to influencing the laws it enacts and the policies it adopts. An interest group is an organization of people who have common interests and goals.

Because government is involved in so many areas of life in 20th-century American society, many interest groups are political. That is to say, they attempt to influence the behavior of government in public policy matters of concern to their members. Since gun policy in the United States is made not at a single point in the governmental system but, rather, at the national (federal), state, and local levels, and within these levels at different branches of government, the groups that have concerns about gun matters attempt to influence government at each point where government has power to make gun policy.

The nature of interest group participation in American political life—not only in shaping gun policy but in shaping other policies, such as education, health, welfare, trade, and environmental protection—involves lobbying (informing government officials of the concerns of a group and attempting to enlist their support), supporting candidates who favor the policies of a group, giving campaign contributions to those candidates, and influencing public opinion. Rival groups with an interest in gun control have been heavily involved in all aspects of gun policy.

As mentioned in Chapter 1, the groups that are most active opponents of gun control are the NRA, the Citizens Committee for the Right to Keep and Bear Arms, the Second Amendment Foundation, and Gun Owners Incorporated. Both the Citizens Committee and Gun Owners Incorporated are even more militant (extreme) than the NRA. The increasing militancy of the gun lobby has sparked the birth in the mid-1970s of an anti-gun movement with the formation of such groups as HCI and the National Coalition to Ban Handguns.

Politically, the NRA is the most powerful organization opposing gun control, and HCI is the leading advocate of the gun control position. Because the NRA is the organization that is the oldest and most influential of groups involved in gun control policy, the debate on p. 80 focuses on the role of that organization in the political process.

Although most people today think of the organization as devoted exclusively to gun control issues, that is not the case, and that was not the case in 1871 when William Conant Church and George Wood Wingate, Union veterans of the Civil War, founded the organization. These ex-military men believed that the Civil War showed that in fighting ability, Southerners had an advantage over Northerners because Southerners had greater firearms experience than Northerners. Church and Wingate set out to improve the marksmanship skills of Americans. The NRA sponsored target shooting competitions. Early in the 20th century, Congress funded NRA shooting matches. After World War II, the NRA emphasized its hunting programs in response to the wishes of many new members who had served as soldiers during the war. Until the 1960s, the main goals of the NRA were firearms safety education, marksmanship training, and shooting for recreation.

Although the NRA had been involved in gun control issues as early as 1911 and was active in influencing the National Firearms Act of 1934 (dealing mostly with weapons used by gangsters) and the Federal Firearms Act of 1938 (requiring federal licensing of gun dealers, manufacturers, and importers), it was not until the 1960s that the organization focused on gun control issues. Gun control issues dominated the work of the organization in the late 1960s in response to public demands to regulate the possession and sale of guns. These demands were sparked by the assassinations of prominent political leaders, such as President John F. Kennedy, Dr. Martin Luther King, Jr., and Senator Robert Kennedy, and to a popular awareness of guns in an increasing number of violent crimes throughout the United States.

The NRA leadership supported some gun control reforms. For example, NRA executive vice president Maxwell Rich told Congress: "On the Saturday night special, we are for [banning] it 100 percent. We would like to get rid of these guns." He testified that those guns have no sporting purpose and are frequently poorly made.

Conflict in the organization between what became known as the Old Guard, favoring the organization's emphasis on marksmanship, hunting, and safety training, and the New Guard, favoring the organization's emphasis on preventing gun control, grew stronger in the 1970s. Complaining that the leadership was too moderate, some members called for a redirection of the organization's policies to a stronger opposition to gun control. The more militant members rebelled against the old-timers in 1977 and took over the organization.

The rebellion was called "The Cincinnati Revolt" because the transfer of power occurred at an NRA convention in that Ohio city, and Harlon Bronson Carter became head in 1977. With this change in policy direction, the NRA became, in the words of writer Osha Gray Davidson, "more than a rifle club. It became the Gun Lobby."

Soft Judges
Make
Hardened Criminals s

Citizens Committee for the Right to Keep and Bear Arms • Liberty Park • 12500 .E. Tenth Place • Bellevue, WA 98005 • (206) 454-4911

INSURED BY
THE
SECOND
AMENDMENT

Citizens Committee for the Right to keep and bear arms • Liberty Park • 12500 N.E Tenth Place • Bellevue, WA 98005 • (206) 454-491

CRIMINALS PREFER
UNARMED VICTIMS

The NRA distributes bumper stickers such as these at conventions to voice its strong opinions on gun control issues.

According to Davidson: "The new NRA would be devoted single-mindedly—and proud of the fact—to the proposition that Americans and their guns must never, never be parted."

Today, the NRA is not only a lobbying organization against gun control; it is a recreational organization, as well. For example, it gives courses on safe hunting and firearms safety. And it was until 1994 the National Governing Body for America's Olympic shooting team.

However, it is as a lobby that the organization has become well known. The NRA has a lobbying arm, the Institute for Legislative Action (ILA), and a political action committee, the Political Victory Fund (PVF). (A political action committee is a group that collects money from its members and contributes funds to candidates and political parties.) The ILA was founded in 1975, and the PVF was founded in 1976. The ILA motivates membership to pursue anti-gun control efforts in legislative matters at the national, state, and local levels. It also sends out fund-raising letters. The PVF gives campaign contributions to candidates supporting its position.

Today, the NRA is a highly visible interest group because it speaks out on issues of crime and gun use—subjects that have generated immense controversy since the 1960s. It takes strong stands on every gun control issue, most notably the Brady Handgun Violence Prevention Act, banning Saturday night specials or semiautomatics, restricting the sale of so-called "cop-killer" bullets, and local handgun bans. That the NRA is influential is widely recognized by both supporters and opponents of the organization. But observers differ about how much power the organization possesses.

DEBATED:

IS THE NRA'S REPUTATION AS A POLITICALLY POWERFUL ORGANIZATION EXAGGERATED?

Yes. The NRA is clearly a powerful organization. But it is not as powerful as it pretends to be. In the 1990s, particularly, it has suffered some stinging defeats. It has been severely battered, and its power is in decline.

Membership and money. A close look at the membership and money of the NRA shows that reports about the strength and wealth of the organization are exaggerated. The organization was financially strong in the 1980s. But a new group of leaders took over the organization in 1991 with a commitment to launch an aggressive membership campaign and increase spending on fighting gun control legislation at the federal and state levels.

Between 1991 and 1995, according to a *New York Times* story in 1995, the organization accumulated cash deficits (losses) of $55.3 million. With corrections made for accounting adjustments, the deficit was $71.9 million. Moreover, the organization sold off some of its reserve funds (money set aside for future or special use), which dropped from $91 million in 1990 to $41 million in 1994. Most of that $41 million was pledged to a collateral (security) on a loan. The collateral was for a loan that the organization obtained to purchase new headquarters in Fairfax, Virginia, just outside of Washington, D.C.

Even the organization's gains in membership are nothing that the organization's most devoted followers should cheer about. Annual membership dues in the period of expansion were $25. But according to financial information that the organization supplied to the Internal Revenue Service and information presented to the NRA finance committee, the NRA spent about $87 to recruit each new member during this period. (In its literature, the organization claimed that it spent only $24 to recruit each new member.) To make matters worse, only 43 percent of the new members renewed their membership. The organization slowed down its membership drive in the spring of 1995. Moreover, some reports indicated that after the Oklahoma City bombing in 1995, the NRA membership numbers were in decline.

The *New York Times* reported in 1995 that according to a confidential letter written by Max W. Goodwin, chairman of the NRA finance committee, the NRA's spending policies had damaged the future strength of the organization. If the financial condition of the organization is as bad as reports indicate, then the power of the organization, which is based in part on its ability to pay for lobbying, political campaigns, and public relations operations, is in decline.

Legislation. Although the NRA has won some major legislative victories, it has suffered some defeats, too. These defeats have been at different levels of government.

Particularly since 1968, the federal government has passed several laws dealing with gun control, and the tide is moving toward gun control. In the 1990s, the pace of federal government activity has picked up. In 1993, Congress passed the Brady Bill, and in 1994, it passed an assault weapons ban. (See Chapter 7.) These were mighty achievements and succeeded in the face of NRA opposition.

The popular outcry for gun control, sparked by some particularly brutal gun incidents, has increased legislative support for gun control. For example, in the aftermath of the Colin Ferguson shootings on the Long Island Railroad, all three Republican members of Congress from Long Island voted for the ban on some semiautomatic weapons in 1994.

Because of its great successes in getting candidates for the House of Representatives and Senate favorable to its position elected to Congress in 1994, the NRA hoped to get legislation adopted that would repeal the assault weapons ban. But the NRA received bad publicity and came under attack because of its strong opposition to the ATF.

The bad publicity arose after the Oklahoma City bombing. Although the NRA condemned the bombing, the news media played up the organization's fund-raising letter attacking the ATF as "jackbooted government thugs," a term used to associate the officials with the police of a dictatorship. Timothy McVeigh, a key suspect in the bombing, had been a member of the NRA for four years, and this fact was highlighted as were some links between the NRA and local militias that were antigovernment in general and anti-federal law-enforcement agents in particular. (These local militias were not the state militias but were rather private organizations that formed for improving military skills. Some private militias were composed of extremist groups.) The uproar over the Oklahoma City bombing and the links to the NRA caused the Republican leaders in the House and Senate to put off their plans to have the assault weapons ban lifted.

The NRA has suffered setbacks at the state and local levels, too. In 1988, Maryland passed a law banning the manufacture and sale of Saturday night specials in the state. It was the first state to ban these weapons. The NRA tried to have the law reversed by getting a referendum on the ballot to that effect. (A referendum allows the people directly, rather than the legislature, to approve or disapprove a proposal. If a majority approves, it becomes law.) Although the NRA spent a considerable amount of money—far more than its opponents—the ban on Saturday night specials was strongly approved by a vote of 58 percent to 42 percent.

Many states had passed waiting-period laws on the purchase of guns even before the Brady Law was enacted. Many states had passed assault weapons bans, too. Some states, such as New York, passed strict laws on gun ownership. In 1990, New Jersey passed the toughest ban on assault

So far, there are no laws restricting the sales of hunting firearms such as a rifle.

weapons. In 1993, Virginia limited to one gun the number of guns a person could buy in that state in one month—a step that was taken because Virginia had become a leading arsenal for criminals throughout the United States. The NRA fought the ban on handguns proposed in Morton Grove, Illinois, in 1981. The ordinance required gun owners to surrender their handguns. The NRA challenged the ordinance in court—but it lost.

The NRA is clearly on the defensive. It must spend its resources to fight what may best be described as a holding action in an effort to keep the situation from changing to the advantage of gun control advocates.

Political campaigns and elections. The power of the NRA to influence electoral outcomes is much less than the NRA would like political candidates and the nation to believe. The "success" of the NRA in elections is based on the fact that the organization usually gives money to candidates who run in "safe districts"—that is, districts in which a candidate who has been elected before continues to be reelected, often with a substantial majority of voters. When the NRA endorses such a candidate, it is generally backing a sure winner anyway. It takes credit for victory where credit is not deserved only to create the illusion of power.

The NRA has lost some widely publicized elections, too. In 1990, Minnesota's Rudy Boschwitz lost his campaign for the U.S. Senate, although he had NRA campaign money. And even in the 1994 congressional elections in which the Republican party seized control of both the Senate and the House of Representatives, two strong opponents of gun control in the House of Representatives—Democrats Jack Brook of Texas and Jolene Unsoeld of Washington State, were defeated.

Popular support. The NRA and its cause are losing popular support. The decline in popular support stems from a great public awareness of the danger of guns to American society, increasing differences with law-enforcement officials, and an unwillingness on the part of the NRA leadership to make compromises in their extreme position.

Americans have become increasingly alarmed over the bloodbath that guns produce each year. They have become more aware of the new weapons that shoot bullets faster and more accurately than older weapons. Highly publicized incidents, such as the killings in Killeen, Texas, and Stockton, California, have produced popular outrage, which has been turned into gun control legislation.

Public opinion polls have revealed popular support for bans on assault weapons and Saturday night specials. The fact that Congress passed the

Brady Bill and the assault weapons ban is a reflection of growing popular support for government action on gun control.

The NRA has lost the support of some of its traditional allies, most notably the police. For years, the NRA was active in supporting the police, but its position against banning "cop-killer" bullets that could pierce bulletproof vests, against plastic guns that might evade detection at airports, and against assault weapons that could cause massive killings led to sharp criticism by some police organizations.

Worse for the NRA was its increasing opposition to federal agents, most notably ATF. It was John Dingell, an NRA board member and a Democratic congressman from Michigan, who in 1981 made the comparison between the ATF and the Nazis in an NRA documentary, *It Can Happen Here*. "If I were to select a jackbooted group of fascists who are perhaps as large a danger to American society as I could pick today, I would pick the ATF," he said.

In 1981, the NRA tried to abolish ATF by encouraging the government to transfer its firearms, explosives, and arson regulation and enforcement personnel to the Secret Service, which is also under the control of the Treasury Department. But the NRA reversed its position when it decided that the Secret Service would be a greater danger to the NRA cause than ATF.

The NRA has been taking some public relations losses particularly because of two shooting incidents. The first was an August 1992 shootout between federal agents and Randy Weaver at his cabin in Idaho. In that incident, Weaver's wife and son were killed. The second incident involved a tragic event in Waco, Texas. ATF agents came to serve a warrant on David Koresh, the head of the Branch Davidian religious cult, at its compound in Waco on February 28, 1993. The ATF believed that the Koresh group had collected a large number of weapons, including machine guns and explosives. A shootout resulted, taking the lives of six cult members and four ATF agents. The ATF withdrew. But on April 19, the FBI shot tear gas into the compound, and the compound was set ablaze, resulting in the death of 80 Branch Davidians. The FBI blamed the cult for setting the fire, although the matter is in dispute.

The bombing of the Alfred P. Murrah Federal Building in Oklahoma City undermined support for the NRA, although there was no direct link between the Oklahoma City bombing and the NRA. The explosion in Oklahoma City, however, focused attention on the entire gun issue, and particularly on the NRA.

For some people who are committed to owning guns, the Waco and Randy Weaver shootings instilled fear that the U.S. government might have a campaign to ban the owning of guns. The seizure of illegal guns was an issue in both cases.

The NRA has come under attack from its most famous supporters, most notably Ronald Reagan and George Bush. On March 29, 1991, former President Reagan said: "I am going to say it in clear, unmistakable language: I support the Brady Bill and I urge the Congress to enact it without further delay." He also said, "I don't believe in taking away the right of the citizen to own a gun for sports, hunting, or their own personal defense.... But I do not believe that an AK-47, a machine gun, is a sporting weapon." And George Bush, another lifetime member of the NRA, resigned from the organization. In the aftermath of the Oklahoma City bombings, he condemned the criticisms of federal agents made by the organization.

Representative John Dingell resigned his post as a board member of the NRA. Announcing his resignation on the House floor, he said, "The only way they can lobby is through threats and intimidation." Even Senator Dennis DeConcini, a Democrat from Arizona, received condemnation from the NRA after he supported the ban on some assault weapons. Prior to that support, the NRA had named him the organization's "man of the year."

Opposition to the NRA comes not only from outsiders but also from NRA insiders. The opposition is in part an indication of the differences among NRA members. NRA members are split between the sport shooters and dedicated Second Amendment supporters. Some hunters want the NRA to return to its sporting purposes, such as promoting marksmanship, gun collecting, and other forms of gun-related recreation.

Some state NRA units are directly challenging their national leaders. Former NRA board member Dave Edmundson organized a State Association Coordinating Committee, which became critical of the leadership of the organization. It accused the NRA of losing major legislative battles and spending members' funds unwisely. The NRA has indeed been losing money. It has cut back on services to members, for example, reducing the frequency of publishing its magazine American Rifleman.

Several magazines even refused to take some of the more extreme NRA advertisements in the 1980s in spite of the fact that the magazines lost revenue for this refusal. Among these were Audubon, Better Homes and Gardens, Ebony, McCall's, and Modern Maturity. Also, some television stations refused to run NRA ads. After the Oklahoma City bombing, Richard Riley, who was the NRA president from 1990 to 1992, evaluated the popularity of the organization. "It's scary.... We were akin to the Boy Scouts of America... and now we're cast with the Nazis, the skinheads, and the Ku Klux Klan."

★ ☆ ★ ☆ ★

The NRA is not the mighty power it used to be. The American people are aware of the organization's activities and reject its message. In this regard, a 1995 *U.S. News & World Report* poll in May 1995 revealed the following:

> Would you be more likely or less likely to vote for a candidate endorsed by the National Rifle Association?
>
> More likely: 23 %
>
> Less likely: 42 %
>
> No difference: 26 %

The American people are alert to the issues of gun control. And the polling evidence shows that NRA support is a drawback rather than an advantage to candidates for public office. The poll is part of the bigger story of an organization in decline.

No. As the leader of the "gun lobby," the NRA has grown in power so that it is one of the most influential political interest groups in America. Its power is based on the NRA's money, organization, tactics of its leaders, and the single-minded dedication of its more militant members.

Membership, money, organization, and allies. The NRA owes much of its political power to the size of its organization, its wealth, and the support it gets from the gun manufacturing industry. As the organization became more militant, the number of its members increased. At the time of the Cincinnati Revolt in 1977, it had 1 million members. Its membership rose to 2.6 million in 1983, and 3.4 million in early 1995.

Much of the money that the NRA takes in from dues, contributions, and other sources is spent on lobbying efforts. The organization's ILA spent $17.7 million in 1991, but thanks to a vigorous effort, spent $28.3 million in 1994.

The NRA launched its "Refuse to Be a Victim" program in order to recruit women.

Because NRA members are particularly alert to issues affecting the possession of guns, the organization can easily mobilize its members for political action. One effective technique is the use of direct mail campaigns in which a group sends letters directly to individuals with a request for contributions or for some form of participation in achieving the goals of the organization. The NRA organizes its members to write letters and make telephone calls to legislators who agree with the NRA view of gun matters. It encourages its members to turn out at meetings in which they can confront local, state, or federal officials threatening their interests in guns.

The NRA is what is known as a "single-issue group." In such a group, as its name suggests, members are dedicated to one issue, and they are likely to act politically largely in terms of that single matter. That is to say, they are so set on that issue that they will write letters, campaign, attend meetings, and vote for candidates who support their single issue. Often, single-issue groups have more power than larger and wealthier groups that have many

What Would Mom Think Now?

It's a different world today, than when you grew up. The pace is quicker, the challenges greater and personal security is a very real issue.

Today, many women are including a LadySmith® handgun as part of their personal security plan. The LadySmith is the first handgun designed for women, featuring slimmer grips, shorter reach and a lighter trigger pull. So whatever your preference, revolver or pistol, there's a LadySmith for you.

LadySmith fits your lifestyle as well as your hand.

interests. Members in these larger groups may lack the intensity of commitment to a cause felt by members in single-issue groups. When they vote in elections, they tend to divide their votes for candidates based on considerations of a variety of issues rather than one single issue.

The NRA makes campaign contributions to political candidates who agree with its views. According to Common Cause, a group that favors political reform and is concerned with the financing of political campaigns, the NRA was the ninth largest contributor among political action committees in the 1992 federal elections. In the 1994 election, its financial contributions helped elect a Republican Congress, which was more friendly to its point of view than the Democrats.

In the 1994 election, moreover, the NRA helped defeat House Speaker Thomas S. Foley and Representative Jay Inslee, Democrats who voted for the assault weapons ban as part of the Violent Crime Control and Law Enforcement Act of 1994. It was pleased with the defeat of handgun ban measures on the ballots in Milwaukee and Kenosha, Wisconsin. With a Republican takeover of Congress, it could look forward to the support of Orren G. Hatch of Utah, the new chairman of the Senate Judiciary Committee and a friend of the NRA. The Judiciary Committee is the Senate unit that considers gun control legislation.

The NRA has won the support of many Presidents. Among its members were Presidents Dwight Eisenhower, John F. Kennedy, Richard Nixon, Ronald Reagan, and George Bush. (As mentioned earlier, however, Bush resigned his lifetime membership in May 1995 in disapproval of the organization's literature attacking law-enforcement officials.)

The NRA has a close relationship with the firearms industry. The NRA and the gun manufacturers and dealers who benefit from the NRA's activities have been clever at gaining new members for the organization. The NRA, for example, recognized that women are a potential market for recruiting, and geared their advertising message to playing on the fears of women about rape and random violence. The NRA estimates that the number of women who now own firearms could be as high as 20 million.

The NRA launched a safety program, "Refuse To Be a Victim" targeted at women. NRA ads depicted a fearful woman as she and her daughter walked through a dark public garage. To furnish women with the weapons that they think they need, gun manufacturers have designed weapons for

In 1989 Smith & Wesson marketed the LadySmith, a handgun designed specifically for women.

President Clinton signs the controversial Brady Bill on November 30, 1993, while former White House press secretary James Brady looks on.

women. In 1989, for example, Smith & Wesson, a gun manufacturer, announced its "LadySmith Program," which was directed at women.

Josh Sugarmann observes: "In 1990, eight percent of the NRA's budget—more than $7.4 million—came from industry ads placed in NRA publications. During the 1960s, when membership and revenues were far lower, advertising at times accounted for more than a quarter of the NRA's budget."

It is not surprising that there is a close link between the NRA and the firearms industry. If laws are weak or nonexistent on gun control, people find it easy to purchase firearms. The stronger the NRA, the more prosperous is the firearms industry. Recognizing that the fortunes of the NRA and the gun industry are linked, the NRA supplies membership application forms to gun manufacturers to include in the packaging of weapons. *American Rifleman* and *American Hunter*, NRA publications, print reviews of firearms. And the NRA annual meetings feature weapons displays from major firearms manufacturers.

Legislation. The NRA has had a long-term involvement with legislation dealing with guns. The organization's early interest in such laws, however, was not in gun control matters, but rather in gaining privileges that reduced the costs of shooting. In 1905, Congress passed a law authorizing the sale of surplus military firearms and ammunition at cost (without the government making a profit) to rifle clubs that met the regulations of the National Board for the Promotion of Rifle Practice, a government unit created in 1903 to build rifle ranges for civilian use and to promote their use. The law provided that the NRA had to sponsor the rifle club for it to be eligible to purchase the firearms and ammunition at cost. By 1910, the military gave away surplus rifles and ammunition to rifle clubs. Two years later, Congress funded the yearly NRA shooting matches.

It was not until the 1930s that the NRA became involved with federal gun control laws. It opposed proposed laws that would regulate many firearms. But it supported the National Firearms Act of 1934 and the Federal Firearms Act of 1938. (See Chapter 7.) The leadership of the NRA supported the Gun Control Act of 1968, which banned the interstate shipment of certain firearms and strengthened the federal government's role in gun control. (See Chapter 7.) The NRA gave this support because the people who ran the organization were of the sportsmen type. Many NRA members were more critical of gun control than the leadership, however. And, as mentioned earlier, the organization became more involved in fighting gun control proposals in the 1970s. The NRA's impact on legislation reflected its increasing power.

Although federal gun control laws have been enacted since the Gun Control Act of 1968, often the final form in which they were passed showed changes from the original bills so as to weaken the final legislation in a manner that made the laws more acceptable to the NRA. The NRA weakened the federal gun law of 1986 by easing some of the gun control regulations of the Gun Control Act of 1968.

The NRA had an influence on the Brady Bill. The Brady Handgun Violence Prevention Act, signed into law in 1993, provides for a five-day waiting period for a person to purchase a gun. But this provision lasts for only five years at which time a system based on an "instant check" through computers will allow the dealer to determine instantly whether a would-be purchaser of a gun is legally eligible to buy the gun. If that person is eligible, then he or she may buy a gun on the spot without waiting the five days.

In a similar way, gun control advocates cheered when the assault weapons ban was enacted. But the ban had so many loopholes that gun dealers could easily avoid the intent of the legislators who wrote the law. The law did not cover many kinds of assault weapons. Gun manufacturers sold models of guns that were only slightly modified from a banned gun so as to get around the law but still be legal.

As these two cases show, gun control advocates won the headlines when the Brady Bill and the assault weapons bill were passed. But the gun control advocates won only the battle, and lost the war.

The NRA never gives up. Even after it is defeated, it rises from the dead. For example, the NRA lost out when the Brady Bill was passed in 1993. A provision of the Brady Bill required a background check and waiting period for anyone reclaiming a gun from a pawnshop. But in 1994, Congress passed a crime bill, which, in effect, canceled that provision.

The NRA has been a powerhouse in lawmaking not only at the national level but at the state and local levels, as well. For example, the NRA succeeded in defeating a referendum in Massachusetts in 1976 that would have banned all handguns in the state.

In 1982, gun control advocates succeeded in getting Proposition 15 on the ballot in California. It would have banned the sale of new handguns, limiting the number of pistols and revolvers in the state to those owned on April 30, 1983. Gun control forces lost heavily when Californians rejected the proposition by 63 percent to 37 percent.

To be sure, the NRA does not win all of its battles at the state and local levels. Morton Grove, a community outside of Chicago, passed a law banning handguns. But after Morton Grove, the NRA began a campaign for state preemption laws. A preemption law restricts local government from enacting laws tougher than its state laws. Before Morton Grove, only three states had passed preemption laws. As of June 1994, 42 states had these laws. The preemption power has been an important weapon at fighting gun control. For example, in 1995, Georgia passed a preemption law that instituted an "instant check" system to prevent felons from obtaining guns. The preemption law overturned ten local waiting periods, including a 15-day waiting period in Atlanta.

Political campaigns and elections. One way to conclude that the NRA's reputation for power is not exaggerated is to look at the power of the organization in political campaigns and elections. The NRA has been able to mobilize its followers and financial resources to oppose candidates who are unfriendly to its cause and to support candidates who are friendly. In 1970, for example, Senator Joseph Tydings of Maryland lost his bid for reelection. He was an advocate of gun control, and the NRA took credit for his defeat.

Some observers reported that the defeat was caused by factors other than the influence of the gun lobby. But as former HCI chairman Pete Shields observes: "Nonetheless, the pistol lobby claimed full credit. As a result, since then the phrase 'Tydings Syndrome' has been heard on Capitol Hill, which means that if you support any form of gun control, the NRA and other gun zealots may come after you."

NRA power in elections continued long after Tydings had gone down to defeat. The NRA played a major role in the defeat of Michael Dukakis in the 1988 presidential election. The organization endorsed George Bush, who won the election by a large majority.

Pete Smith, a member of the House of Representatives from Vermont, was a supporter of the NRA. He was a Republican party moderate who supported Democrats on some issues. He was also an opponent of gun control, but he favored the Brady Bill and a ban on assault weapons. The NRA targeted him in the 1990 elections. It defeated him, too. Bernie Sanders, a mayor of Burlington, won Smith's seat. Sanders was an opponent of the Brady Bill and the assault weapons ban. Some political analysts say that opposing the NRA in a district that is anti-gun control can cost a candidate between three to eight percentage points in an election.

Since state and local governments also enact gun control laws, NRA political involvement in campaigns is not limited to the national government. Robert Roberti, a California Democrat in the California State Senate, led an assault ban law through the state legislature. His opponents drew up a recall petition.

Recall is a procedure for removing an elected official from office before his or her term ends. When a certain number of citizens (depending on state and local laws) sign a recall petition, a special election is held. If the majority of voters in a recall election favors the recall, the official loses the job and is replaced by someone chosen on the recall ballot or in a later election. Roberti's opponents received enough signatures to require a recall election—only a half year before his term was to expire. The NRA poured in $60,000 to punish Roberti.

Although Roberti survived the recall, he paid a price. He had to spend $800,000 in fighting the recall—money he planned to spend in a campaign for state treasurer. "The recall drained me," he said. "I think that was one of their [the NRA's] objectives. It cost me the whole war chest. It also prevented me from campaigning in other parts of the state because I was tied down in my own district." For its part, the NRA asserted that its only goal was to respond to its constituents (residents of an elected official's district).

All but two of the 27 new members elected to the House of Representatives of the Washington State legislature carried top ratings from the NRA in the election of 1994. The NRA claimed that in the 1994 elections, 20 of 25 NRA-endorsed candidates won governorships, and 74 percent of NRA-backed state legislative candidates won offices.

In the 1994 elections, the NRA spent $3.2 million to support candidates friendly to the NRA's positions on gun issues. Almost all of the candidates it supported won. Politicians understand that if they challenge the NRA, they risk the opposition of a powerful organization and possible defeat at election time.

Popular support. The NRA has a lot more support from the American people than its critics say. A *U.S. News & World Report* poll in May 1995 asked a key question:

> Do you view the National Rifle Association as friendly to or in conflict with the goals of you and your family?
>
> Friendly to: 46 %
>
> In conflict: 39 %

On some key issues identified with the NRA, moreover, public opinion is equally supportive. The polls show that the public does not favor a complete handgun ban, a position advocated by some gun control groups. In many cases where the people have a chance to vote directly in a referendum, a majority of voters support the NRA position.

No one doubts that the NRA has problems. But the extent of these problems has been exaggerated. The NRA remains a powerful force that will success-fully resist or weaken gun control legislation in the years ahead.

Chapter 7
GUNS AND GOVERNMENT REGULATIONS

Debate: Are Handgun Bans, Waiting Periods, and Mandated Added Penalties for Illegal Gun Use During the Committing of a Crime Effective Gun Control Measures?

The United States has more gun laws than any other country in the world, with about 20,000 local, state, and federal laws on the subject. The laws, however, are less restrictive than gun control laws in many other Western countries.

The earliest gun control laws in America predate independence from Great Britain. The first gun control law was in Colonial New England, when the Colony of Massachusetts prohibited the carrying of defensive arms in public places. In the 19th century, several states passed laws banning the carrying of concealed weapons, with Kentucky being the first such state in 1813.

The first laws enacted on gun control in Virginia prevented African Americans from owning guns. The purpose of targeting African Americans was to prevent them from rebelling against slavery. Even after the Civil War ended the practice of slavery, in 1865 and 1866 several Southern legislatures adopted "Black Codes" denying the right to bear arms to African Americans. Congress overrode the Codes in 1866 with the enactment of the Civil Rights Act and in 1868 with the ratification of the Fourteenth Amendment. This amendment gives the federal government responsibility for guaranteeing equal rights under the law to all Americans.

But Southern legislatures devised clever means of denying firearms to African Americans through banning handguns and requiring the registration of handguns. The registration requirements were applied to African Americans, not to Caucasians.

African Americans were not the only group of Americans denied firearms. Federal law prevented the sale of arms and ammunition to Native Americans described as "hostile." It was not until 1979 that the federal government lifted its restrictions on the sale of firearms to Native Americans. Some Southern states passed gun control laws to disarm union organizers. Before the 1890s, Northern states had few laws banning the open carrying of firearms. But beginning late in the 19th century, such laws were enacted there. Northern states turned to firearm restrictions as a response to fears of radicals, labor unions, and immigrants.

The National Firearms Act of 1934 was in direct response to the wide use of machine guns by gangsters in the 1920s.

But it was not until the state of New York passed the Sullivan Law (named for Timothy D. Sullivan, a New York City political leader who was active in getting it passed) in 1911 that a strict comprehensive state law was adopted. It came about as a result of growing criminal and domestic violence in New York City. The Sullivan Law requires an individual to obtain a permit to purchase, own, and possess a handgun. A local authority has power to deny or revoke a permit based on criminal behavior or questionable reputation.

Today, state and local laws vary considerably. For example, in 1981, the town of Morton Grove, Illinois, a suburb of Chicago, passed an ordinance banning machine guns, sawed-off shotguns, and handguns. (See Chapter 6.) The law does not affect law-enforcement officials, members of the armed forces, licensed gun collectors, and gun clubs in which the guns are kept on the club's premises.

In contrast to Morton Grove, in 1982, Kennesaw, Georgia, a city 24 miles northwest of Atlanta, enacted a law requiring the head of every household in the town to "maintain a firearm, together with ammunition therefore." The law does not include residents with a physical or mental disability that would prevent them from using a firearm, heads of households who are paupers (extremely poor people) and cannot afford firearms, people with religious or philosophical convictions against possession of a firearm, and convicted felons.

Federal laws regulating guns are a development of the 20th century. The 1919 War Revenue Act places a manufacturer's tax on arms and ammunition to help pay the costs of U.S. participation in World War I. The Firearms in the Mails Act of 1927 bans the mailing of concealable firearms to private individuals. The National Firearms Act of 1934 was directed against weapons used by gangsters. It requires the registration of machine guns and sawed-off shotguns.

The Federal Firearms Act of 1938 (FFA) was the first attempt to regulate interstate and foreign commerce in firearms and ammunition. The law requires firearms manufacturers, importers, and dealers to obtain annual licenses from the Internal Revenue Service.

The shipment of weapons to anyone other than a licensed dealer or manufacturer in states that require a permit to purchase is banned. The law also outlaws the shipping of firearms and ammunition to persons convicted of or under indictment for a crime punishable by more than a year in prison, or a fugitive from justice. According to Josh Sugarmann: "The law was, unfortunately, easy to circumvent [get around]—those in proscribed [prohibited] categories merely lied. In the 30 years following enactment of the FFA, there was only one conviction of a purchaser for violating his state's permit law."

The Gun Control Act of 1968 bans the importation of Saturday night specials from foreign countries. The federal law does not ban the importation of handgun parts. These parts can be assembled in the United States onto frames made in the United States. Domestic production and the assembling of weapons increased from 60,000 in 1968 to a million in 1970.

In 1986, the Firearms Owners Protection Act (McClure-Volkmer Amendments—named for Senator James McClure, Republican from Iowa; and Representative Howard Volkmer, Democrat from Missouri) amended the Gun Control Act of 1968 by allowing for the legal interstate sale of rifles and shotguns as long as the sale is legal in the states of the buyer and seller. The act eliminates some record-keeping requirements for ammunition dealers, eased licensing requirements for individual dealers who do not regularly trade in guns, permits gun dealers to engage in gun sales at gun shows, and prohibits the establishment of a comprehensive firearms registration system. It also makes it illegal for a person to own or transfer a machine gun that was not lawfully manufactured and possessed before the 1986 law was signed. In 1988, the Undetectable Fire-arms Act (known as the "plastic gun" legislation) banned the manu-facture, import, possession, and transfer of firearms not detectable by security devices.

The Brady Handgun Violence Prevention Act of 1993 requires law-enforcement officials to make constant background checks of prospective purchasers. After five years from the time the law was enacted, the waiting period is to be replaced with a system of instant checks to determine whether the prospective buyer has legal restrictions (for example, the person is a felon) that prevent him or her from buying the handgun.

President Clinton signed into law the Violent Crime Control and Law Enforcement Act of 1994. One provision of that bill bans for ten years the manufacture, sale, and possession of 19 types of assault weapons and "copycat" versions of those guns. It also bans some guns with two or more features associated with assault weapons. But it specifically excludes from the law 650 types of semiautomatic weapons.

Although the federal government has expanded its involvement in gun control matters since the 1930s, it keeps out of many regulatory matters. As mentioned in Chapter 3, the CPSC assures safety on products, such as toys, cars, and kitchen appliances, to prevent injury and death to the unsuspecting public. But firearms and ammunition, which cause death and injury to thousands of Americans, are exempt from the law. (The commission has jurisdiction over non-powder firearms, such as a BB gun, however.)

Firearms are regulated by the ATF. Unlike some other regulatory agencies, such as the Food and Drug Administration and the CPSC, ATF has no power to set standards and recall defective products. ATF has some limited control over imported firearms because of federal government legislation imposing a "sporting purposes" test written to prevent the importation of Saturday night specials and surplus military rifles and shotguns, but it has practically no control over domestic firearm design and production.

Federal and state laws vary considerably on gun control, and some classification is necessary to evaluate the large number of laws on the subject. Some classifications are:

Place and manner restrictions: for example, a ban on carrying of weapons in particular areas or in a concealed manner.

Tough penalty for use in a crime: a punishment that adds time to a sentence when a crime is committed with a gun.

Ban on some kinds of individuals from owning guns: for example, felons, drug addicts, and mental patients.

Licensing: Permissive licensing requires individuals to apply for a license or sometimes apply but comply with a waiting period. For restrictive licensing, a person who wants to own a gun needs to furnish a reason for owning it in order to receive a license. Mandatory (required) licensing means that an applicant has a right to a license unless the person is legally forbidden to possess the license because of some specified reason. Discretionary licensing means that the applicant must prove to an authority that he or she has a "reasonable need" to own and carry a concealed handgun.

Registration: The owner of a gun needs to provide information about the gun he or she owns.

To say, then, that one favors gun control means to make a general statement about the need for government regulation of guns. But the actual gun control policies vary considerably from place to place. It becomes essential in a discussion of gun control to focus on specific proposals for changing gun control law.

DEBATED:

ARE HANDGUN BANS, WAITING PERIODS, AND MANDATED ADDED PENALTIES FOR ILLEGAL GUN USE DURING THE COMMITTING OF A CRIME EFFECTIVE GUN CONTROL MEASURES?

Yes. The damage that guns produce in the United States is so great that drastic measures must be taken to stop the bloodshed. Handgun bans, waiting periods, and mandated added penalties for illegal gun use during the committing of a crime are effective gun control measures.

Handgun bans. Handguns are the weapons that are most involved in crime involving firearms. If the nation enacts a federal handgun law, we will sharply reduce the amount of gunshot killings and woundings.

It is not enough to look at state laws, which differ substantially. Critics of handgun control point to the District of Columbia, which has the strictest handgun control law in the United States but which suffers from a high rate of gun crimes. What is ignored, however, is that a resident of the District of Columbia has no difficulty in going over a bridge to reach neighboring Virginia, where the gun laws make it much easier for a person to buy a firearm than the gun laws in the District.

The situation in New York State is equally instructive. In 1911, the Sullivan Law made it a felony (serious crime), rather than a misdemeanor (criminal offense less serious than a felony) to carry a concealed weapon without a license. According to Pete Shields:

Probably because the Sullivan Law was extremely tough, especially as amended over the years, a Treasury Department study in the early 1970s (Project Identification) showed that over 90 percent of the handguns used in crime in New York came from out of the state. It was the same old picture: because there is no federal law, once a state passes a stringent handgun law, the handguns begin to flow in from states where there are weak laws. For example, the handgun used to kill John Lennon [the former Beatle in 1980] was acquired in Hawaii and that used to kill former Congressman Allard Lowenstein [in 1980] came from Connecticut.

Just how significant out-of-state handgun use is in supplying handguns to criminals can be seen from the experience of Virginia. That state used to be known as the gunrunning capital of America and was a prime source for drug dealers, gang members, and other criminals in the North.

In July 1993, a law went into effect in Virginia restricting the number of handgun purchases per person to one a month in that state. Using facts from ATF, the Center to Prevent Handgun Violence, a research arm of HCI, reported in August 1995 that guns seized by police in the Northeast were traced to Virginia only half as often since the one-gun-a-month law was enacted. That is to say, that of all guns seized in the Northeast that originated from the Southeast, only 16 percent came from Virginia since the law went into effect, compared with 35 percent before then. Handgun control laws make a difference, as this study shows.

Banning a particular kind of gun may be highly effective. In 1934, for example, the federal government banned machine guns. Very few machine guns are used in crime today. Less than one percent of all homicides involve the use of a machine gun. If there is a success story, it is the ban on machine guns. We will have more success stories when we ban handguns.

Critics of handgun control make the "slippery slope" argument, namely, that once government bans handguns, it will proceed down the slippery slope and ban all kinds of guns. Such a view is alarmist. If that kind of effect would occur in the enactment of laws, there would be no laws on anything. One could argue that a ban on drinking while driving could lead us to ban all alcohol consumption, but such an argument would lack credibility. A specific ban on handguns will not necessarily lead to a total ban on all guns.

One particular benefit of a handgun ban would be that it would remove the Saturday night specials from the streets. That gun is inexpensive and generally of low quality. Because it is so cheap to purchase, too many of these guns are around and can only cause unnecessary bloodshed.

Waiting periods. Waiting periods are popular throughout the United States, and rightly so. At the time that the Brady Bill was enacted, at least 25 states had already imposed restrictions on handgun purchases similar to Brady.

Waiting periods make much sense for three reasons: First, law-enforcement officials need to be certain that a prospective purchaser of a firearm would not be a threat to the community. By establishing a waiting period for sales, the system will uncover criminals who seek to obtain weapons through legal channels. This is not to say that waiting periods will find all such people or even most such people, but it is to say that some people who might otherwise have weapons will not have them.

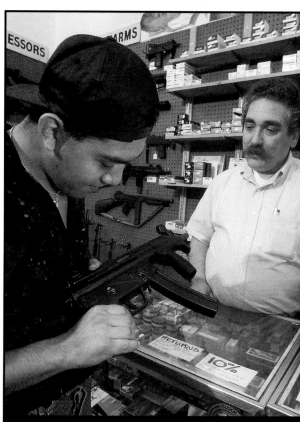

Second, a waiting period is useful for people who, because of some psychological disturbance, feel that they need to run out and buy a gun. Such people include someone who is angered by the behavior of a loved one (such as the break off of a romantic relationship or an announcement of an intention of divorce) or despondent because of some personal setback (such as the failure to get a job at a company or a high grade at college).

Third, law-enforcement officials are capable of locating felons or other dangerous people in this manner. Thanks to the wonders of modern technology, most notably the computer, law-enforcement officials have greater access to reliable information that they can call up

Waiting periods to purchase firearms enable law-enforcement officials to assess whether a prospective buyer, such as this one, might pose a threat to the community.

quickly than was the case just a few decades ago. The waiting period is a useful tool, then, for keeping some weapons out of the hands of people who, when armed with guns, are dangerous to the community.

Waiting periods are successful. Between 1989 and 1993 computerized background checks or similar waiting period programs in California, Florida, Virginia, and Maryland blocked more than 47,000 attempted purchases by persons who at the time were banned from buying firearms. The checks in Virginia and Florida helped not only screen out prohibited individuals but revealed hundreds of fugitives wanted for other crimes, as well.

California has a waiting period that is longer than the Brady Law calls for. In 1991, 500,000 requests were made to purchase guns. The state stopped nearly 6,000, including 3,000 involving buyers with assault records and 34 with homicide records.

The Brady Handgun Violence Prevention Act, too, has been extremely successful in achieving its goals. A year after the law was passed, up to 45,000 convicted felons, or 2 to 3.5 percent of all applicants for handguns, were turned down after the application reviews, according to surveys conducted in 1995 by ATF, CBS News, and the International Association of Chiefs of Police in association with HCI. Moreover, the experience of states shows that one to two percent of applicants for gun purchases were turned down as a result of background checks.

District Attorney J. Tom Morgan of DeKalb County, Georgia, which includes part of Atlanta, said, "I believe the Brady Bill has reduced the number of crimes those felons would have committed." He added: "It shows criminals do go to stores to buy guns, and they obviously don't buy handguns to go duck hunting."

One should not overestimate the importance of waiting periods. "I don't think anybody sees it as making a major dent in the violent crime problem," said Philip J. Cook, an economist and expert on gun violence at Duke University who is sympathetic to gun control. "It's not going to reduce the murder rate by 20 percent." Cook added: "But it's not very costly, and it's not going to be a major imposition on gun buyers. It's a common-sense type of regulation, and it's going to help on the margin."

Added penalties. An added penalty for using a gun in a crime removes the decision making from prosecutors and judges in cases where guns were used in committing a crime. Such mandatory sentences prevent courts and prosecutors from being too lenient with people who are willing to commit crimes with guns. These sentences also serve as a deterrent to criminals when considering a crime.

There are too many criminals out on the streets. Too often the prison is a revolving door because a person who has committed a crime is charged with a less serious offense. The legal term is known as plea bargain and means that a person who commits an offense agrees to plead guilty to a lesser offense with the understanding that the penalty will be less than a guilty verdict on the more severe offense would call for.

Prosecutors can tell the public that they are fighting crime by citing the number of convictions that they obtain. But often the convictions are plea bargains, and the criminal is soon right back on the street. This legal procedure allows criminals who use guns in their crime to benefit, too, and the consequence to society is horrible.

By removing decision making on penalties from prosecutors and judges, gun-toting criminals will be in prison where they belong. Most importantly, criminals might get the message and might be deterred in some cases from committing serious violent crimes. The public can only benefit from such a reform.

No. No one questions the fact that guns have produced considerable damage in the United States and that drastic measures must be taken to stop the bloodshed. But handgun bans, waiting periods, and added penalties for illegal gun use during the committing of a crime are the wrong ways to deal with the problem.

Handgun bans. A handgun ban will create more problems than solutions. We know what happens when we ban things that people want. We banned the sale of alcohol in the 1920s and produced a criminal market for illegal liquor. We have tough laws on the possession and sale of hard drugs, but we have lost the "war on drugs" that politicians announce from year to year. Moreover, we know both from prohibition of alcohol and the criminalization of hard drugs that we have increased the prospects for corruption among our public servants. This situation occurs because some police and other government officials accept bribes from criminals selling these illegal products in return for ignoring such unlawful activities.

If we ban handguns, then people will find a way to get them in the same manner that they obtain other illegal items that they want. They will smuggle guns into the country, and they will even produce homemade guns. Already in many cities where permits are required to have guns, many citizens carry guns illegally for self-protection. There is little doubt that people will do what they think they have to do to get guns in spite of the law.

In 1976, the District of Columbia passed one of the strictest handgun laws in the nation. The law prohibits the purchase and possession of handguns by civilians in the District of Columbia unless a citizen already owned a handgun and registered it by 1976. But the city has been dubbed "the murder capital of America" because of the large number of gun fatalities that occur there.

If gun control laws are supposed to reduce crimes, then they have failed. New York State adopted the Sullivan Law in 1911. But, as sociologist James Wright notes: "New York City alone constitutes about 20 percent of all armed robberies anywhere in the nation in an average year, and accounts for about 13 percent of all the nation's violent crime."

The example of the "success" of the Virginia law limiting the sale of handguns to one per person per month (see page 102) is based on faith in gun control rather than on facts. As Tanya Metaksa, chief lobbyist for the NRA, points out, the federal statistics used in the study were unreliable because they trace guns seized by police that were not necessarily used in crimes. The real reason why gun seizures were down in the Northeast is because tougher law enforcement and sentencing has served as a deterrent to violent crime.

The real victims of the Virginia law are honest, law-abiding citizens. As Metaksa notes about these citizens: "They're now deathly afraid that if they go to try to buy a gun inadvertently because they don't keep track of the days, they get caught into being a criminal unintentionally."

Advocates of handgun control often do not spell out the details of their plan. A close look at some of the details, however, might raise some doubts about how the policy would be carried out. For example, when gun controllers say that they favor gun control, they often do not include private police in that control. But if private police are included, then rich people will be able to purchase their security by hiring a private police force armed with handguns for protection. Poor people, in contrast, who cannot afford to hire private police will be left defenseless.

The slippery slope argument should not be exaggerated, and gun control advocates are correct to point out the dangers of taking an argument to an extreme. But the slippery slope argument has considerable force particularly as applied to guns, as it has been to other highly condemned products, such as alcohol.

The temperance movement began in the United States in the 19th century as an effort to limit alcoholic consumption but resulted in a total prohibition of consuming alcohol, with the adoption of the Eighteenth Amendment in 1919. The registration of handguns in New York City through the Sullivan

Law led to abolition of handguns for many New Yorkers. In Great Britain, gun registration led to the virtual abolition of handguns. For both New York City and Great Britain, the first steps were moderate enough. But supporters of change were really interested not in making moderate changes, but rather in making major changes, and succeeded in getting their way.

Some countries have engaged in mass confiscations of weapons. Gun registration lists were used in mass confiscations in Greece, Bermuda, and the Irish Republic, for example.

The slippery slope argument is convincing when we observe the behavior of HCI, the leading U.S. gun control organization in the United States. HCI claims that it wishes to regulate—and not outlaw—the use of guns. But it supported the total ban on handguns in Morton Grove, Illinois. As head of HCI and wife of James Brady, who had been severely injured in the assassination attempt on President Reagan, Sarah Brady is not satisfied with the Brady Handgun Violence Prevention Act she helped get Congress to enact. Pleased with her success with the Brady Law, she calls for a Brady Bill II, which would go further than Brady Bill I. If she is successful, there will no doubt be Brady Bills III, IV, and V until all guns are made illegal.

It is wrong to use the success in banning machine guns as a model for banning handguns. The reason why the machine gun ban is successful is not because the ban works, but rather because of the limitations of the weapon itself. The machine gun is large and difficult to control. Machine gun fire often misses its target and endangers bystanders.

Handgun banners focus on the Saturday night specials for their particular scorn. Most criminals do not use Saturday night specials in their crimes. The evidence indicates that people have these weapons mostly for protection. Outlawing Saturday night specials would disarm the poor and have little impact on criminals. It would make the poor more likely to become victims of crime. Critics of Saturday night specials cannot argue that Saturday night specials are dangerous in the hands of criminals but useless for defensive purposes by potential victims.

Finally, a handgun ban would probably increase the purchase of handguns in the weeks before coming into force, as has happened on other such occasions. For example, sales of handguns doubled just before the Gun Control Act of 1968 went into effect. And brisk sales of all kinds of guns were made before the Brady Bill became law.

Waiting periods. The case against waiting periods may be made with three arguments. First, few felons try to get guns through legitimate gun dealers.

Unfortunately a waiting period would not have prevented John Hinckley, Jr. (above) from shooting former President Ronald Reagan and James Brady.

Most get guns "on the street," or from a family member or friend, or they steal them. To focus on the few felons stupid enough to try to buy a gun legitimately is a waste of valuable law-enforcement time.

Many of the worst gun incidents of recent years were not, or would not have been, prevented by a waiting period. Patrick Purdy (see page 7) bought his guns in spite of a 15-day waiting period. Mark David Chapman, John Lennon's assassin, bought his gun in Hawaii, a state with one of the strictest waiting periods in the United States. Colin Ferguson purchased his gun legally in California, in compliance with a 15-day waiting period there.

John Hinckley, the man who shot President Ronald Reagan and James Brady, bought his revolver six months before he committed this crime. Had there been a waiting period, he would still have committed the act. And had a check been made on previous convictions or on a history of commitment for mental illness, the results would not have prevented him from purchasing the gun.

The effect of waiting periods is to prevent law-abiding citizens from purchasing guns to protect themselves, their families, and their property. When the Los Angeles riots occurred in 1992, endangered citizens went to gun stores to purchase a firearm. The gun dealers told them to return in 15 days to comply with California's waiting period for all guns. Looters in Los Angeles had a great time taking property that did not belong to them. Some owners of small businesses stood by as they saw their stores being raided and were helpless to do anything about it. Writer David Kopel observes: "After Hurricane Andrew, Florida's looters did considerably less damage than their California counterparts, in part because Florida has only a three-day handgun waiting period, and no wait at all on long guns."

Second, the idea that people who are sufficiently motivated to kill or to be suicidal will be kept from finding a way to commit their acts of violence when they can't buy a gun quickly is far-fetched. One of the most important predictors of a violent domestic crime is previous domestic assaults. "Cooling down" time is not the problem for people with records of assaults. These people have plenty of time to meet the required waiting period of a Brady-type law.

A close look at waiting period law points out some problems in making a waiting period effective. Although the Brady Law prohibits the mentally ill from purchasing a gun, computer checks often cannot locate sufficient records for determining whether a prospective purchaser is mentally ill because the laws of confidentiality protect medical records that contain information about mental illness. It is also difficult to identify illegal aliens and some people with a dishonorable discharge from the military, as the Brady Law requires.

Third, a main fear about waiting periods is that the police will impose their own standards for determining whether to grant permission to sell a gun rather than those fixed by law. In the past, police departments have used laws according to their own judgment to impose greater restrictions on acquiring guns than many legislators who wrote the gun laws intended. It is possible, and even likely, that the police would twist a waiting period into a law that would pose unnecessary restrictions on people who need to purchase a gun for legitimate purposes.

It is misleading to cite the number of applicants who were stopped from purchasing a gun as a result of a Brady-type law. The numbers of purchase denials do not tell us what happens after the applicants were denied the right to purchase a gun. Bill Bridgewater, executive director of the National Alliance of Stocking Gun Dealers, a trade group in Havelock, North Carolina, said: "The 40,000 people who were stopped were only stopped at that store at that time. They weren't arrested. So all they had to do was to go out on the street corner at midnight and pay more to get a gun." And James Q. Wilson, a professor of management at the University of California at Los Angeles, commented: "The test is whether felons have been stopped from buying guns and then killing people with them. And that we don't know."

We do not need waiting periods where there are alternatives that can achieve the goal that waiting periods are supposed to produce. These alternatives are an instant phone check on the purchaser's background, creation of a firearms owner ID card, and a card that would add a fingerprint to a computerized driver's license.

Added penalties. Mandatory added sentences for crimes committed with a gun are such a popular idea for solving the gun problem in America that it is no wonder that politicians support it and that both the NRA and HCI favor it, too. But mandatory sentences furnish no practical solution to the illegal use of guns. The problem is that the prisons are crowded now. In addition, judges are already tough with repeat violent offenders.

The United States has the highest rate of incarceration (the placing of criminals in prison) of any developed country in the world. By the end of 1994, the nation's prison population soared to more than a million people. According to a Justice Department report, 958,704 inmates were in state prisons and 95,034 were in federal prisons in 1994. This prison population accounted for only about two-thirds of the nearly 1.5 million people incarcerated in the United States. The remaining one-third were in local jails, which usually hold people who are awaiting trial or serving sentences of less than a year.

The prisons are bulging at the seams. In 1994, eight state systems were so crowded that they sent their inmates to local jails. On average, the federal prisons operated at 17 percent above capacity, and state prisons were at 25 percent over capacity. Nearly 4.9 million people were under some correctional supervision. Of the 4.9 million, 2.8 million were on probation and 671,000 on parole.

The growth rate in prisoners is high, too. At the end of 1980, 1 in every 453 U.S. residents was incarcerated. By the end of 1993, the incarceration rate rose to 1 in every 189. The time spent in federal prison is growing, moreover, because of tougher federal sentencing guidelines. Fox Butterfield, a reporter for the *New York Times*, concludes that if the trend in prison and jail population growth continues, "The number of Americans behind bars or on probation or parole will soon approach the 6 million students enrolled full-time in four-year colleges and universities nationwide."

Add-on sentences for gun crimes while not serving as a deterrent to crime will worsen the problem of overcrowded prisons. People who are committed to killing to achieve their goals of robbery or vengeance face longer penalties for those crimes than the added penalties for gun crimes. If they are not deterred from crime by the tough punishment, they will not be deterred by the weaker punishment. The knowledge that a committed bank robber will face an add-on to a sentence if he or she commits the crime with a gun is less of a deterrent to bank robbing than the law against bank robbing itself.

Handgun bans, waiting periods, and add-on penalties are not practical solutions to the problems that guns pose to American society today. The nation needs to find better solutions, for too much is at stake in the choices we make.

The United States has the highest rate of incarceration of any developed country in the world.

Chapter 8

CONCLUSION: THE FUTURE OF GUN CONTROL

Firearms have been an important feature in American life since the first Europeans settled in the New World. Although most people who use firearms in the United States do so in a peaceful manner, the illegal and violent use of firearms remains a great problem to a civilized society, as does the role of firearms in suicides and accidents.

It would be foolhardy to predict developments about gun control in the years ahead. A more practical approach to considering the entire subject of gun control is to think about the factors that will influence public policy in this matter. Among the most important issues will be the character of public opinion about gun control, views of elected public officials, effectiveness of interest groups, the degree of violent crime and social unrest, and serious, highly publicized incidents involving firearms.

Public opinion. Public opinion in gun matters shifts depending on events. Although U.S. public opinion polls show that the American people believe they have a right to bear arms, they also show support for some kinds of gun control. Public opinion is not always immediately translated into legislation, however, because a strong-willed minority in Congress can prevent a law from being enacted.

But gun control laws have been enacted at the national, state, and local levels. The federal government has been active in the 20th century, with much legislation passed since the Gun Control Act of 1968. Federal legislation, moreover, has been enacted during both Republican and Democratic administrations. State and local governments have led the way in gun control. Some of the laws enacted at the state and local level, such as waiting periods, eventually became federal law.

Gun control advocates have a long list of the kinds of laws that they would like to see enacted. To achieve their goals, they will have to convince large numbers of Americans that their proposals will accomplish the objectives that they claim.

One of the strengths of the NRA is its ability to mobilize members in political campaigns.

Elected public officials. The officials who are elected to public office in a democracy are sensitive to public opinion. They also help to shape public opinion. The prospects for gun control will depend upon the views of politicians committed to this issue and the strength of their commitment.

Neither the Democratic party nor the Republican party is united on the issue of gun control. In general, though, the Democratic party is more in favor of gun control than is the Republican party. The outcome for gun control legislation depends on success in getting people elected to public office who are committed to or opposed to gun control legislation.

Interest groups. The gun lobby, dominated mostly by the NRA, has been a key player in preventing gun control legislation from being enacted or in weakening proposed gun control legislation. Its power comes from its large membership, the intensity of the feeling of its most militant members, its campaign contributions, and its ability to get its members mobilized in political campaigns. The power of the gun lobby has received setbacks, as it has lost the support of key allies, notably elected representatives and groups that were supportive at first. Former President Ronald Reagan endorsed the Brady Bill, and former President George Bush gave up his lifetime membership in the NRA. Police organizations have increasingly opposed the NRA because of the organization's opposition to such legislation as the ban on so-called "cop-killer" bullets and the ban on assault weapons.

The gun lobby also faces opposition from a rising gun control lobby, led most notably by HCI. The gun control groups have increased in membership, financial resources, and political influence. But the gun lobby has survived previous setbacks and achieved some of its objectives over the long haul.

The roles of gun-issue and gun control interest groups will both affect the course of gun control legislation because these groups will influence public opinion and elected public officials. No doubt, each side will win some and lose some of the most hotly debated issues.

Violent crime and social unrest. The struggle over control will be shaped by developments within the society. Calls for gun control grew stronger in the 1960s as the use of guns in violence intensified. As early as the 1930s, the federal government banned machine guns as a response to gangland killings. But gun violence also strengthens the forces opposed to gun control because of the appealing arguments of the need for self-protection.

No doubt the course of gun control will be influenced by social unrest, as the response to the Los Angeles riots of 1992 demonstrates. Gun sales were brisk after the riots. More riots in urban areas would probably lead to more guns, regardless of the laws about gun possession.

Highly publicized incidents. Finally, incidents involving important public figures are bound to have an impact on gun control. The assassinations of John F. Kennedy, Martin Luther King, Jr., and

Sarah Brady, head of HCI, addresses a group of mothers at a rally
in Washington, D.C., on May 15, 1995, protesting against gun violence.

Robert Kennedy led the way to the enactment of the Gun Control
Act of 1968. And some of the assault weapon incidents of the 1980s
led to the enactment of the assault weapons ban in the Violent
Crime Control and Law Enforcement Act of 1994.

★ ☆ ★ ☆ ★

The American people are truly divided on the issue of gun control. It
is possible that both sides of the issue will become so hardened that
they will be unwilling to compromise. The character of the debate

has already become so intense at times that each side looks upon the other as immoral, insensitive, and irrational.

Such a situation may not be dangerous when limited to one issue. The success of the American political system, however, is based to a large degree on the willingness of groups to adjust their positions to challenging groups. On some issues, however, such an adjustment is impossible or difficult to achieve. But when the people of a democracy divide on many key issues in a manner that fails the tests of compromise, the stability of democracy becomes threatened. Only developments of the coming years will reveal the influence that the politics of gun control will have on the strength of American democracy.

ABBREVIATIONS

ATF	Bureau of Alcohol, Tobacco and Firearms
CPSC	Consumer Product Safety Commission
FFA	Federal Firearms Act
FFL	Federal Firearms License
GAO	Government Accounting Office
HCI	Handgun Control, Inc.
ILA	Institute for Legislative Action
NCBH	National Coalition to Ban Handguns
NRA	National Rifle Association
PVF	Political Victory Fund

GLOSSARY

aggravated assault Assault with the use of weapons or threat or use of weapons with the intention of inflicting injury.

automatic A firearm that fires continuously with the pressing of the trigger.

Bill of Rights The first ten amendments of the Constitution.

bootleggers Gangsters who illegally traded in alcohol.

bullet The tip of a cartridge that is loaded into a gun.

caliber The diameter of a bullet measured in decimals of an inch or in millimeters.

cartridge The case that holds the charge for a gun.

clip A container for cartridges.

common law The system of law based on custom and precedent.

constituents Residents of an elected official's district.

Consumer Product Safety Commission The federal agency that seeks to protect the public from unreasonable risk of injury associated with consumer products.

criminologists Students of crime and criminal behavior.

culture The core of traditional ideas, practices, and technology shared by a people.

cylinder The turning chamber of a revolver.

deficits Losses.

deters Prevents or discourages.

double-action revolvers Handguns that can be cocked and fired by a single pull of the trigger.

federal system A form of government in which powers are divided or shared between the central, or federal, government and the states.

gun A mechanical device that throws one or more objects outward, usually through a tube or barrel.

gun control Government restrictions on gun sales, ownership, and use.

handguns Small firearms, with barrels usually varying in length between two and eight inches. They are sometimes called pistols.

incarceration The placing of criminals in prison.

interest group An organization of people who have common interests and goals.

interstate commerce Business or trade between states.

kinetic energy Energy associated with motion.

kitchen-table dealers Gun dealers typically operating out of their homes.

legislative Lawmaking.

lethal Capable of causing death.

lobby A group that attempts to influence the content of government laws and the policies of government agencies.

long gun A firearm meant to be fired from the shoulder.

Mace A liquid used to temporarily blind a would-be assailant.

magazine A container for cartridges.

manually By hand.

militia An armed force of citizen soldiers who may be called to service during emergencies.

obsolete No longer useful; old-fashioned.

paramilitary Relating to irregular military organizations acting as a replacement or substitute for a regular military force.

parliament Legislative body.

pistols See "handguns."

plea bargain A situation in which a person who commits an offense agrees to plead guilty to a lesser offense with the understanding that the penalty will be less than a guilty verdict on the more severe offense would call for.

plinking The shooting of tin cans and natural inanimate targets found in the woods.

political action committee A group that collects money from its members and contributes funds to candidates and political parties.

posse A group of people organized by a public official to assist in law enforcement.

precedent A court decision that is used as a standard to decide similar cases.

preemption law A law restricting local government from enacting laws tougher than its state laws.

psychopaths People with personality disorders.

ratification Formal legal approval.

recall A procedure for removing an elected official from office before his or her term ends.

referendum A procedure that allows the people directly, rather than the legislature, to approve or disapprove a proposal.

repeater A gun capable of being fired several times without reloading.

reserve funds Money set aside for future or special use.

revolver A handgun with a chamber that contains several cartridges that turn.

rifle A firearm with a rifled barrel (spiral grooved bore) fitted with a stock intended to be held against the shoulder. A rifle requires the shooter to pull the trigger for each shot fired.

safe districts Districts in which a candidate who has been elected before continues to be reelected, often with a substantial majority of voters.

Saturday night special Inexpensive and usually poorly made handgun that is easily concealed.

sedition Conduct or language that encourages rebellion against the authority of a country.

semiautomatic A firearm that reloads automatically but requires the shooter to pull the trigger for each shot that is fired.

shotgun A type of long gun that releases pellets with each firing.

single-action revolvers Guns in which one shot is manually loaded at a time before firing.

single-issue group A group in which members are dedicated to one issue and are likely to act politically largely in terms of that single matter.

stocking dealers Commercial enterprises operating storefront businesses to sell guns.

tyranny Dictatorship.

usurpations Wrongful or illegal seizures.

victimization A crime affecting one individual person or household.

BIBLIOGRAPHY

Chapter 1: Introduction: Firearms in America

Anderson, Jervis. *Guns in American Life.* New York: Random House, 1984.

Hofstadter, Richard. "America As a Gun Culture." *American Heritage* 21 (Oct. 1970): 4–11, 82–85.

Kopel, David B. *The Samurai, the Mountie, and the Cowboy: Should America Adopt the Gun Controls of Other Democracies?* Buffalo, NY: Prometheus Books, 1992.

Larson, Erik. *Lethal Passage: How the Travels of a Single Handgun Expose the Roots of America's Gun Crisis.* New York: Crown, 1994.

Nisbet, Lee, ed. *The Gun Control Debate: You Decide.* Buffalo, NY: Prometheus Books, 1990.

Wright, James D. "Ten Essential Observations on Guns in America." *Society* 36 (Mar./Apr. 1995): 63–68.

Zimring, Franklin E., and Gordon Hawkins. *The Citizen's Guide to Gun Control.* New York: Macmillan, 1992.

Chapter 2: Guns and Ammunition

Anderson, David C. "Street Guns: A Consumer's Guide." *New York Times Magazine*, Feb. 14, 1993, pp. 20–23.

Newton, Michael. *Armed and Dangerous: A Writer's Guide to Weapons.* Cincinnati, OH: Writer's Digest Books, 1990.

Rees, Clair F. *Beginner's Guide to Guns and Shooting*, rev. ed. Northbrook, IL: DBI Books, 1988.

Rosa, Joseph G. *Guns of the American West.* New York: Crown, 1985.

Sherrill, Robert. *The Saturday Night Special.* New York: Charterhouse, 1973.

Witkin, Gordon, and Dan McGraw. "How David Koresh Got All Those Guns." *U.S. News & World Report* 114 (June 7, 1993): 42, 44.

Chapter 3: Guns and Crime

Kates, Don B. "The Value of Civilian Handgun Possession as a Deterrent to Crime or a Defense Against Crime." *American Journal of Criminal Law* 18 (Winter 1991): 113–167.

Kleck, Gary. *Point Blank: Guns and Violence in America.* New York: Aldine de Gruyter, 1991.

Newton, George D., and Franklin E. Zimring. *Firearms and Violence in American Life: A Staff Report Submitted to the National Commission on the Causes and Prevention of Violence.* Washington, D.C.: National Commission on the Causes and Prevention of Violence, 1969.

Quigley, Paxton. *Armed & Female.* New York: E.P. Dutton, 1989.

Shields, Pete, with John Greenya. *Guns Don't Die—People Do.* New York: Arbor House Publishing Co., 1981.

Weil, Douglas S., and David Hemenway. "Loaded Guns in the Home." *Journal of the American Medical Association* 267 (June 10, 1992): 3033–3037.

Wilson, James Q. "Just Take Away Their Guns." *New York Times Magazine*, Mar. 20, 1994, p. 47.

Wright, James D., and Peter H. Rossi. *Armed and Considered Dangerous: A Survey of Felons and Their Firearms*, expanded edition. New York: Aldine de Gruyter, 1994.

Wright, James D., Peter H. Rossi, and Kathleen Daly. *Under the Gun: Weapons, Crime, and Violence in America*. New York: Aldine de Gruyter, 1983.

Chapter 4: Guns, Suicides, and Accidents

Kellerman, Arthur L., et al. "Gun Ownership as a Risk Factor for Homicides in the Home." *New England Journal of Medicine* 329 (Oct. 7, 1993): 1084–1091.

_____. "Suicide in the Home in Relation to Gun Ownership." *New England Journal of Medicine* 327 (1992): 467–472.

Kopel, David B. "Children and Guns," in David B. Kopel, ed. *Guns: Who Should Have Them?* Amherst, NY: Prometheus Books, 1995, pp. 309–406.

Sugarmann, Josh, and Kristen Rand. "Cease Fire." *Rolling Stone* no. 677 (Mar. 10, 1994): 30–34, 36–38, 40, 42.

"Violence." *JAMA: Journal of the American Medical Association* 267 (June 10, 1992): 2985–3108 (whole issue).

Witkin, Gordon. "Should You Own a Gun?" *U.S. News & World Report* 117 (Aug. 15, 1994): 24–25, 27–31.

Zimring, Franklin E. "Firearms, Violence and Public Policy." *Scientific American* 265 (Nov. 1991): 48–54.

Chapter 5: Guns and the Constitution

Cottrol, Robert J., ed. *Gun Control and the Constitution: Sources and Explorations on the Second Amendment.* New York: Garland Publishing, 1993. 3 vols.

Cress, Lawrence Delbert. "An Armed Community: The Origins and Meaning of the Right to Bear Arms." *Journal of American History* 71 (June 1984): 22–42.

Halbrook, Stephen P. *That Every Man Be Armed: The Evolution of a Constitutional Right.* Albuquerque: University of New Mexico Press, 1984.

Levinson, Sanford. "The Embarrassing Second Amendment." *Yale Law Journal* 99 (Dec. 1989): 637–659.

Malcolm, Joyce Lee. *To Keep and Bear Arms: The Origins of an Anglo-American Right.* Cambridge, MA: Harvard University Press, 1994.

Mitgang, Herbert. "What Right to Arms?" *New York Times*, May 5, 1995, p. A31.

Stalhope, Robert E. "The Ideological Origins of the Second Amendment." *Journal of American History* 69 (Dec. 1982): 599–614.

Stalhope, Robert E., and Lawrence Delbert Cress. "The Second Amendment and the Right to Bear Arms: An Exchange." *Journal of American History* 71 (Dec. 1984): 587–593.

Chapter 6: Guns and Politics

Alter, Jonathan. "How America's Meanest Lobby Ran Out of Ammo." *Newsweek* 123 (May 16, 1994): 24–25.

Butterfield, Fox. "Aggressive Strategy by N.R.A. Has Left Its Finances Reeling." *New York Times*, June 26, 1995, pp. A1, A12.

Leddy, Edward F. *Magnum Force Lobby: The National Rifle Association Fights Gun Control.* Lanham, MD: University Press of America, 1987.

Spitzer, Robert J. *The Politics of Gun Conrol.* Chatham, NJ: Chatham House, 1995.

Sugarmann, Josh. *National Rifle Association: Money, Firepower & Fear.* Washington, D.C.: National Press Books, 1992.

Trefethen, James B., and James E. Serven. *Americans and Their Guns: The National Rifle Association's Story Through Nearly a Century of Service to the Nation.* Harrisburg, PA: Stackpole Books, 1967.

Weiss, Philip. "The Hoplophobe Among the Gunnies." *New York Times Magazine*, Sept. 11, 1994, pp. 64–71, 84, 86.

Chapter 7: Guns and Government Regulations

Butterfield, Fox. "More in U.S. Are in Prisons, Report Says." *New York Times*, Aug. 10, 1995, p. A14.

Lacayo, Richard. "A Small Bore Success." *Time* 145 (Feb. 20, 1995): 47–48.

_____. "Beyond the Brady Bill." *Time* 142 (Dec. 20, 1993): 28–32.

Sugarmann, Josh, and Kristen Rand. *Cease Fire: A Comprehensive Strategy to Reduce Firearms Violence.* Washington, D.C.: Violence Policy Center, 1994.

U.S. Cong., House. *Brady Handgun Violence Prevention Act.* Hearing before the Subcommittee on Crime and Criminal Justice of the Committee on the Judiciary, 103rd Cong, 1st Sess., 1993.

FURTHER READING

Almonte, Paul, and Theresa Desmond. *Gun Control.* New York, NY: Macmillan Children's, 1995

Barden, Renardo. *Gun Control.* Vero Beach, FL: Rourke, 1990

Biskup, Michael D., ed. *Criminal Justice: Opposing Viewpoints.* San Diego, CA: Greenhaven Press, 1993

Dolan, Edward F., and Margaret Scariano. *Guns in the United States.* Danbury, CT: Franklin Watts, 1994

Edel, Wilbur. *Gun Control: Threat to Liberty or Defense Against Anarchy?* Westport, CT: Praeger, 1995

Gottfried, Ted. *Gun Control: Public Safety and the Right to Bear Arms.* Brookfield, CT: Millbrook Press, 1993

Hawxhurst, Joan C. *The Second Amendment* (Vol. 2 American Heritage History of the Bill of Rights series). Parsippany, NJ: Silver Burdett Press, 1991

Hitzeroth, Deborah. *Guns: Tools of Destructive Force.* San Diego, CA: Lucent, 1994

Kopel, David B., ed. *Guns: Who Should Have Them?* Amherst, NY: Prometheus, 1995

Lindop, Edmund. *Assassinations That Shook America.* Danbury, CT: Franklin Watts, 1992

Miller, Maryann. *Coping with Weapons and Violence in School and on Your Streets.* Baltimore, MD: Rosen, 1993

Newton, David E. *Gun Control: An Issue for the Nineties.* Springfield, NJ: Enslow, 1992

Robin, Gerald D. *Violent Crime and Gun Control.* Cincinnati, OH: Anderson, 1991

Siegel, Mark A., et al. *Gun Control: Restricting Rights or Protecting People?* Wylie, TX: Information Plus, 1995

Steele, Philip. *Terrorism.* New York, NY: Macmillan Children's, 1992

Strahinich, Helen. *Guns in America.* New York, NY: Walker & Co., 1992

Tipp, Stacey. *America's Prisons.* San Diego, CA: Greenhaven Press, 1991

Weksesser, Carol, and Charles P. Cozic, eds. *Gun Control.* San Diego, CA: Greenhaven Press, 1992

INDEX